This book is for Harvey Goldman, who had the incredible foresight to create the Photographic Electronic Imaging major at the University of Massachusetts Dartmouth almost 30 years ago. I use the skills I learned there on a daily basis. I could not possibly have had a more relevant, comprehensive, and enjoyable college education. Thanks for all of that!

It is also for Janine Wong. I wish I had just listened to you during those many patient hours that you tried to teach me graphic design. All these years later it is still the weakest part of my skill set and the skill I look most forward to mastering. Thanks for taking me along on the field trip to Barrett Communications even though I certainly was not one of your best students.

Finally, it is for Julie Townsend, for allowing me to intern at Barrett Communications, kicking off my career, and giving me a chance to work with Nadine Flowers, Lisa Scoville, Tracy Preston Mazzuca, Gabrielle Miranda, Kris Knight, Tony deFigio, Dave Pothier, Jeff Reed, and the rest of the Barrett crew. I miss working with all of you.

From Chaos
to Concept

From Chaos
to Concept

A Team Oriented Approach to Designing World Class Products & Experiences

Kevin Collamore Braun

WILEY

ISBN: 978-1-119-62896-5

ISBN: 978-1-119-62891-0 (ebk)

ISBN: 978-1-119-62900-9 (ebk)

Manufactured in the United States of America

Wiley publishes in a variety of print and electronic formats and by print-on-demand. Some material included with standard print versions of this book may not be included in e-books or in print-on-demand. If this book refers to media such as a CD or DVD that is not included in the version you purchased, you may download this material at booksupport .wiley.com. For more information about Wiley products, visit www.wiley.com.

Library of Congress Control Number: 2020937481

V10019471_062920

ABOUT THE AUTHOR

Kevin C. Braun is the founder of Braun Interactive, a design consultancy located in the heart of the Silicon Valley. Kevin has over 24 years of software design and development experience. The work he has done has helped improve user experiences for world-class companies including Google, Samsung, Rolex, Hyundai, Michael Kors, MIT, Harvard, Cisco Systems, Keurig, and Vermont Teddy Bear. He has also worked with industry leaders in healthcare, insurance, automotive, mobile devices, and consumer goods. Along with his professional experience, he has more than nine years of experience teaching college-level user-centered design and front-end development courses.

ACKNOWLEDGMENTS

First, thanks to my wife Christine and my boys Dakota, Slater, and Colt for putting up with me during the better part of a year while I hid in my office working on this book. I am looking forward to hiking with all of you a lot more now.

I would also like to express my very great appreciation to Devon Lewis for guiding me through the crazy process of authoring a book like this and Lisa Koepenick for all that she did to keep me on track along the way.

Finally, my special thanks to John Need and Barath Kumar Rajasekaran for their tireless editing work.

—Kevin C. Braun

CONTENTS

WHO SHOULD READ THIS BOOK

If you are a designer, developer, product owner, or student looking to get into any of these professions, this book will provide you with the methods and tools necessary to enable your teams to design and build experiences customers love and avoid the primary reasons software projects fail.

By reading this book you will learn how to use goals, strategies, and measurable objectives refined with personas, scenarios, and use cases to create useful, usable, and beautiful user experiences. This book covers both UX strategy and execution and will help your company not only improve top-line revenue by creating products users love, but also improve the bottom line by creating operational efficiencies.

I wrote this book with multiple readers in mind. It is written so that it could be read cover to cover for those who want to learn the entire process, or alternatively it can be used as a resource that readers pull off the shelf when guidance is needed on a specific topic. The key concepts are discussed multiple times in different contexts throughout the book to help ensure that all readers are exposed to the most valuable information regardless of their reading style.

This Book Covers

- Making sure that what you are working on is useful and valuable to your users before you spend time and money making it usable and beautiful

- How to make sure your system is usable before you spend time and money making it beautiful

- Tips for designing beautiful solutions so that they will represent your brand well and help users scan, read, comprehend, and complete tasks more efficiently

- Elements of coding the experience so that it is developed to maximize accessibility and performance

- Making sure your team can measure the performance of your solutions and use data to drive the direction of your next iteration

- Ensuring that your iterations and product roadmap are aligned around what will provide the most value to your users and your company

- Making sure these methods and tools have the best chance to succeed within your organization

Reader Support for This Book

Companion Download Files

As you read through the chapters in this book, many of the example artifacts you will encounter are available for download from www.chaostoconcept.com.

How to Contact the Publisher

If you believe you've found a mistake in this book, please bring it to our attention. At John Wiley & Sons, we understand how important it is to provide our customers with accurate content, but even with our best efforts an error may occur.

In order to submit your possible errata, please email it to our Customer Service Team at wileysupport@wiley.com with the subject line "Possible Book Errata Submission."

INTRODUCTION: THE GOLDEN BUTTER KNIFE

Imagine watching a user experience (UX) research session. In this session a participant is eating a bowl of cereal while a researcher like myself is observing them as they try to complete their task. This type of research is called a *contextual inquiry*, but don't worry too much about that now. We'll go into the details later. The most important thing to know about this imaginary research session is that the participant eating cereal is using a butter knife to scoop the cereal from the bowl instead of a spoon.

Obviously using a butter knife isn't as efficient as using a spoon because the milk and cereal are continually falling off the knife instead of being transported to the participant's mouth. In this case, we can measure the amount of time it takes for the participant to eat a bowl of cereal, and we could create a benchmark called "time on task." We can use that benchmark later in our process to measure whether our changes have improved the experience or made it worse.

In this example, it's easy to see that the butter knife is the wrong tool for the job. The participant is performing the wrong interaction. The fact that we know what is wrong makes it obvious how we should fix the problem. Changing the interaction by providing the participant with a spoon will reduce the participant's time on task and improve the cereal eating experience.

When designing software products, the real-world issues that product, design, and development teams encounter are harder to identify than the issues discussed in this butter knife example. The real-world issues being harder to identify is the primary reason many software design and development teams are spending large amounts of money and time specifying, designing, and developing a beautiful, expensive, industry-leading butter knife using the best materials possible instead of creating a simple recyclable spoon.

This is a painful reality for many product teams all over the world. These misdirected efforts are producing refined products that do not improve the experience for the user, and because the product teams do not have the necessary visibility into the root cause of the issues, they do not understand why their product is floundering in the market.

Using the processes outlined in this book, your team will have the skills needed to know that a poorly designed recyclable spoon will provide a better user experience than an exquisite solid gold butter knife. They will also know that the improved experience will likely lead to higher revenue and less expensive material costs, resulting in an improved bottom line by creating operational efficiencies.

MAKE IT USEFUL

"There is nothing worse than a crisp image of a fuzzy concept."

—Ansel Adams

What Are We Trying to Do and How Will We Know If We Did It?

Being able to clearly articulate what a team is expected to do and what the desired outcomes are is the first step on the road to success. That sounds obvious, but I've been in countless kick-off meetings where neither of those two questions could be answered by the project stakeholders. The leadership teams had some vague statements to share about the high-level direction such as "Improve the UX" or "We want to be the Apple of our industry," but nothing that is specifically actionable.

This isn't just my observation. According to an article published in the *MIT Sloan Management Review*, "Only one-quarter of the managers surveyed could list three of the company's five strategic priorities. Even worse, one-third of the leaders charged with implementing the company's strategy could not list even one." (sloanreview.mit.edu/ article/no-one-knows-your-strategy-not-even-your-top-leaders)

If you try to shoot the flock you won't hit anything. You need to pick a goose and target it specifically. The same thing is true in business. The first thing you need to do to succeed is to identify and document your goal.

In contrast, one customer of mine came to me with a very specific goal. They knew from their analytics that customers who bought specific products had higher average order values (AOV). Their goal was to increase the number of visitors to their site that purchased those specific items.

With that clearly focused goal in mind, I researched how their competitors were attempting to solve the same problem. In this specific case everyone seemed to be doing the same thing, so there wasn't any inspiration to be found. Since I couldn't find anything helpful while reviewing the competition, I completed a "clicks to complete" assessment to quantify the complete task from start to finish. A clicks to complete assessment simply measures each click required to complete a specific task or use case. Knowing the number of clicks (or interactions) it takes a user to complete a specific task can help identify issues and help validate potential solutions.

In the original version of their site this task took 50 clicks to complete. I could tell from my evaluation that there were a few big problems. The first and biggest problem was that the existing user flow required the user to jump back and forth between different types of tasks. This can cause users to lose context and abandon the process. The second was that all those clicks increased the user's "time on task" and the longer it takes users to complete a task, the more likely it is that they will get sidetracked.

After verifying both of those issues via their usage analytics, I began exploring options for how we might eliminate the loss of context and reduce the number of clicks to complete. I figured if we could do that, we would likely see an increase in our conversion rate and average order value Key Performance Indicators (KPIs).

My initial efforts were focused on reducing the loss of context. To do that I reviewed various interaction pattern libraries (www.welie.com/patterns and www.patternfly .org/v3) in search of inspiration for something that would eliminate the need for users to move back and forth through the process multiple times to complete their transaction.

In the end, I decided on a wizard-based user flow so that users could complete subtasks one at a time and move through the process step by step. Wizard interfaces break down complex user flows into individual screens for each step. This allows the user to focus on one task at a time and also provides space in the interface for more instructions. That solved the first problem and also reduced the number of clicks significantly but created screens that were a bit dense with form fields. When I first tested those wireframes with some coworkers, they mentioned that seeing all those form fields that needed to be completed in the new design was intimidating. They were right.

This is the same problem that Disney has in its theme parks. If visitors could see the actual length of the line they would need to wait in to be able to get on the ride, they might choose to not even try. As the amazing design book *Universal Principles of Design* points out . . . to solve that, Disney uses a technique called "progressive reveal." All that really means is that Disney hides a lot of the line from view by including the line in the building that houses the attraction and zigzags the line so a visitor only ever sees the first group of people instead of the entire line. The actual length of the line gets progressively revealed as the user moves through the process.

Seeing only the first part of the line is less intimidating, so visitors are more likely to get in the line. Once they are there, they become more and more invested in staying in the line because of the time they have already invested in being there in the first place.

I decided to go back to the whiteboard and incorporate the progressive reveal technique into my design by using the accordion interaction pattern with the wizard interface I created. An accordion interface provides summary data for each element that needs further review. The first element that needs input is expanded so the user can complete the required interactions, while the others are collapsed in order to save space and not overwhelm the user. This approach reduced the number of form elements the user sees, making it more likely that users will start the process. Once they start the process, they start building an investment of time and become less likely to abandon it.

Once I had a clickable prototype of the new accordion/wizard hybrid interface ready, I tested again with more coworkers because we didn't have a budget to test with users. It wasn't ideal, but testing with people even if they are not a direct match for your user demographic can be better than not testing at all especially if the system you are working on is used by the general public.

This new interface reduced the clicks to complete by 50% and eliminated the loss of context issue that the previous version had, so I was pretty confident that testing would go well.

The coworkers were able to complete the tasks well and didn't have any further feedback, so we moved this solution on to development.

This entire process, from the first meeting where the team discussed what they found in the analytics until the new interactions went live on the site, took only two months and cost less than $35K in development costs. Immediately after this solution went live, we saw an increase in conversions and an estimated $9.00 increase in average order value. At that rate, it only took a few days of orders to pay for the entire effort, and the rest of that AOV increase going forward has created a very healthy return on the investment.

There was only one designer and one contract developer on this project, and a lot of the larger user experience design process was missing from this effort due to time and resources. You don't need a multimillion-dollar budget and a team of hundreds to make a real impact on your business. The first things you need are a clear goal and the knowledge of how you will measure your progress along the way.

Creating a Constitution for Your Project—The Framework That Empowers the Team

Choose your own adventure . . . do you want to read another anecdotal story to help provide context for the material that follows? If so, just keep on reading. If not, skip to page 5.

The road to vaporware is paved with tradeshow promises.

If you have been in the software business for very long, it's likely you have been there. It's tradeshow season and nothing else matters but getting something together that will help the sales team demonstrate enough new value in your product to justify the cost increase the board of directors is trying to cram down everyone's throat. Everyone is in a tough position.

The product people know they are the ones who are supposed to find this new value and articulate it in terms of a plan that can be executed in some overly aggressive time frame. It doesn't take too long for the product team to start "thinking different" and eventually come up with some ideas that sound great in the echo chamber, but in reality would take at least five years of time to develop *if* it was actually the right direction in the first place.

The designers know they are rushing the process and that everything they are doing is based on the assumptions of the C-level folks and the product team instead of being vetted with user testing and/or market analysis because there simply isn't enough time. They also have a sneaking suspicion that the elaborate screens they are creating for the demo likely include functionality that is basically impossible to build. That said, they have the power of Sketch and InVision to make all these terrible ideas look fabulous.

Then there are the developers. They have lived this cycle so many times it barely fazes them. They are about to be handed a nightmare and be wedged firmly between an ambiguous design spec full of dubious assumptions and a rock-solid tradeshow deadline.

The dev team pulls together an entirely rigged demo full of holes and fake data with the promise from the leadership team that after the tradeshow we'll take some time to "do this right," refactor, and in general create a viable product.

To help avoid many of these problems modern software teams face, I leverage goals, strategies, objectives, and tactics to establish consensus and protect the team from needless pivots, sprint injections, or otherwise being derailed.

In order for this to work you need to invite decision makers from the product, development, UX, design, research, and QA teams to a workshop where you will define your goals, strategies, and objectives together. I'll explain how to do this in the next chapter but for now, just know that consensus is essential at this phase and also know that it is OK if you don't have members of all those teams. The core team, or as some companies call them, "squad," should include members of the product, UX, and development teams to ensure that your plan has buy-in from the teams most connected to the building of your product or service.

Once the squad has created the constitution for the project the squad can protect it effectively to ensure it stays on track.

If the head of sales comes back from a tradeshow with customer feedback that "has to be addressed immediately," members of the squad can refer to the constitution for the project and ask what objective of the project this customer request will positively impact. If there is a compelling argument that this new idea will help achieve an existing objective, the team can consider shifting priorities. If there is no compelling argument to be made, then add this new idea to the backlog to be revisited when the current objectives have been addressed. This isn't to say that the constitution cannot be amended, because there are circumstances in which it will be necessary. This process simply helps to make sure changes in direction are not taken lightly and that voices from key team members are heard as part of the process.

Goals, Strategies, Objectives, and Tactics—The Plan the Team Will Work From

Once you recognize the need for a unifying plan for your teams, you will need to begin the process of getting enough buy-in from your organization to justify the time needed for the initial workshop.

Over the years I've learned that opinions are not worth very much. If you base your business decisions on opinion the best you can hope for is tentative cooperation, but there will always be those that naysay your plans and undermine your team's ability to work as a cohesive unit. When leading from your gut instincts it is also more likely that you will lead your team in the wrong direction.

Data and information provide a solid foundation to make observations. Using data to back up your decisions also provides a defensible position for recommendations you make for your team. It's not always possible to use data to make every decision, but you should try to whenever possible.

The first rule of buy-in is inclusion. In my experience people are far more likely to fall in line with a plan that they were involved in from the start and when their voice has been heard as part of the process. A wonderful side benefit of including the team in the process is that you will likely also uncover more insights and identify more robust solutions.

The first step is to reach out to the key members of your organization with a Monday morning email asking them to take 15 minutes to document their understanding of the biggest challenges facing your business. See the following sidebar for an example.

> Hi <name>,
>
> We are kicking off a user experience project for our organization and would like to include your feedback in the process. If you can, please take 15 minutes before the end of the day Wednesday to reply to this email with a list of what you see as the biggest issues currently facing our business.
>
> Feel free to reach out with any questions you have,
> <your name>
> <your contact info>

Once you have as many responses as possible on Thursday morning, create a spreadsheet and do the analysis required to remove the duplicates and then prioritize the issues the team identified. The list of issues you documented will serve as a great starting point for your workshop.

When you are done you should have something that looks like Figure 1.1.

The next step is to create a workshop agenda that can be used to help participants better understand what to expect, and hopefully get them excited about being part of a process that has been proven at some of the world's biggest and most profitable organizations. I use a spreadsheet to kick off the process of creating my agendas. In the end, the final product is usually a slide deck that gets used during the workshop but the spreadsheet is a fast way to document the process and iterate on content, timing, and presenters. The spreadsheet is also helpful as an artifact that can be shared with your team to gather feedback and get approval.

When I'm done with my first pass at a workshop agenda, it looks a lot like what you'll see in Figure 1.2.

You can find a link to the agenda spreadsheet template here:

www.chaostoconcept.com/workshop/agenda

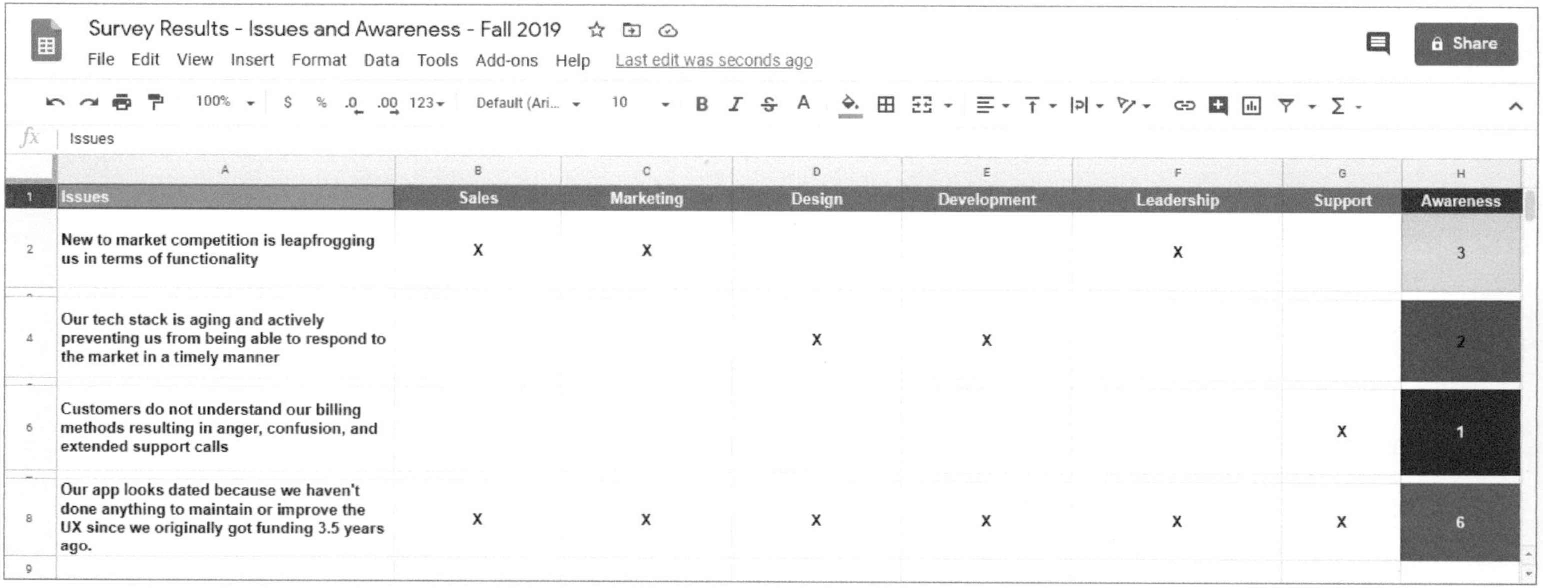

Survey Results – Issues and Awareness – Fall 2019

File Edit View Insert Format Data Tools Add-ons Help   Last edit was seconds ago

Issues	Sales	Marketing	Design	Development	Leadership	Support	Awareness
New to market competition is leapfrogging us in terms of functionality	X	X			X		3
Our tech stack is aging and actively preventing us from being able to respond to the market in a timely manner			X	X			2
Customers do not understand our billing methods resulting in anger, confusion, and extended support calls						X	1
Our app looks dated because we haven't done anything to maintain or improve the UX since we originally got funding 3.5 years ago.	X	X	X	X	X	X	6

Figure 1.1: An Issues and Awareness Document can help expose your team to issues they were previously unaware of while acting as a discussion starter for a priority-setting exercise.

Workshop, Day 1 – Feb 2, 2020						
Est Time/Hrs.	Agenda Item	Description	Location	Deliverables	Team	Optional
8.45 AM	**Continental Breakfast**		3rd Floor Great Room			
9:00am – 9:30am	**Kick off**	1. Welcome 2. Team introduction 3. Reviewing the goals of the workshop 4. Reviewing agenda	3E	Meeting Notes	Kevin Lisa Nadine / Tracy Tony Julie	Kris Gabrielle
9:30am – 10:00am	**The Goal Driven Design Process**	Review how goals, strategies, and objectives serve as the foundation of our design process	3E	Meeting Notes	Kevin Lisa Nadine / Tracy Tony Julie	Kris Gabrielle
10:00am – 10:45am	**Company and Goals**	Understanding company and goals 1. High level business goals 2. Business goals for this project 3. Sales positioning: How does your sales team sell? 4. Organizations within(i.e. Sales, Marketing, Product, Design, Engineering) 5. Success metrics	3E	Initial GSOT Document	Kevin Lisa Nadine / Tracy Tony Julie	Kris Gabrielle
10:45am – 11:00am	**Break**					
11:00am – 12:00pm	**Review Study Findings**	Review findings from study and how they correlate with assumptions / information	3M	Research Study Report	Kevin Lisa Nadine / Tracy Tony Julie	Kris Gabrielle
12:00pm – 1:00pm	**Lunch**		LUNCH DELIVERED			
1:00pm – 2:30pm	**Review Competitive Usability Analysis**	Review competitive usability analysis and how it correlates with assumptions / information	3M	Competitive Review Report	Kevin Lisa Nadine / Tracy Tony Julie	Kris Gabrielle
2:30pm – 2:45pm	**Break**					
2:45pm – 3:45pm	**Develop Strategies**	Discuss and document any current and newly identified strategies related to the stated business goals	3M	Updated GSOT Document	Kevin Lisa Nadine / Tracy Tony Julie	Kris Gabrielle
3:45pm – 4:00pm	**Wrap-up**	Discuss Day 2 agenda Wrap-up		Meeting Notes		

Figure 1.2: Workshop agendas help participants prepare and keep the team on track.

Once you have a solid draft, it's a good idea to share it with a small set of key team members to get some feedback. Use their feedback to create a final draft version and use that as part of your invite to the workshop.

Let the participants know that a draft agenda is attached to the invite and make sure they are aware of what the goals of the workshop are along with what their time commitments will be. I find that this is a good time to also include a link to Human Factors International's quick video on the ROI of UX. If you have some doubters in the mix, that video will hopefully convince them that the time invested in this process will be worth it. The video in combination with your thoughtfully prepared agenda should prove to be pretty compelling:

www.youtube.com/watch?v=094kYyzqvTc&t=160s

Once you have the workshop scheduled and have at least members of the core team (a product team leader, a UX team leader, a dev team leader, and hopefully an executive that will act as the voice of the C-level) confirmed as participants, you can go on to create your workshop presentation slide deck.

A slide from my presentation deck might look something like what you'll see in Figure 1.3.

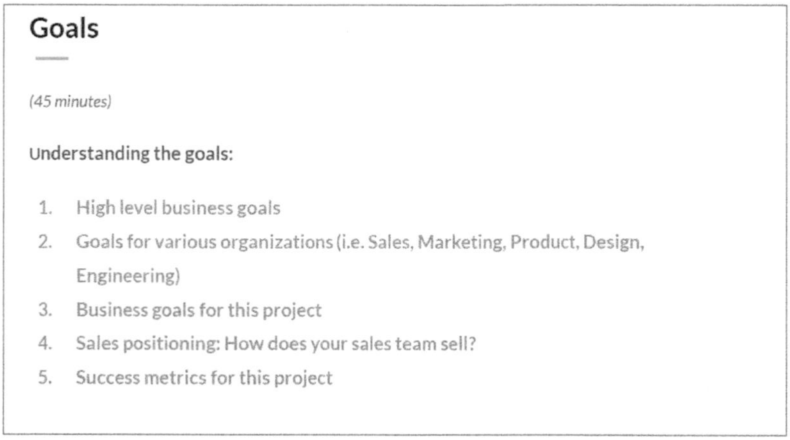

Goals

(45 minutes)

Understanding the goals:

1. High level business goals
2. Goals for various organizations (i.e. Sales, Marketing, Product, Design, Engineering)
3. Business goals for this project
4. Sales positioning: How does your sales team sell?
5. Success metrics for this project

Figure 1.3: A simple slide deck helps participants follow what's being presented and gives presenters a place to showcase support materials.

You can find a link to a template of my deck at www.chaostoconcept.com/workshop/sides.

Once you have your slide deck prepared, it's a good idea to walk through the process with a trusted colleague if this is your first time doing something like this. It will help you become more familiar with the process and will also help ensure that what you have planned will lead to the desired outcomes.

In this workshop it's very important that your outcomes include:

- **The high-level goal of the project.**

  An example of a goal might be to sell more of a specific product or service because this will increase a metric like average order value (AOV) or conversion rate.

- **The strategies that are identified as being likely to help achieve that goal.**

  A strategy for the defined goal might be to make it easier for users to find the product. Another strategy might be to provide more information about the product on the product detail page (PDP) so users can compare products more easily and feel more confident in their choices, making it more likely they'll complete a transaction.

- **The measurable objectives required to be able to execute on each strategy.**

  An example of an objective could be updating product descriptions with specific keywords so that the search algorithm will surface the target product in more search results, making it easier for users to find. Objectives need to be measurable so you can easily report on whether or not this objective has been met. In this case we could measure this objective by documenting that we need to update the descriptions of 10 key products with at least 5 new keywords that have been identified as key search terms via the site's usage analytics.

  The spreadsheet illustrated in Figure 1.4 shows what a Goals, Strategies, Objectives, and Tactics (GSOT) artifact might look like. If something the team is considering conflicts with the GSOT document, that topic should be put in the icebox for later consideration or the team will need to meet to agree on amending the GSOT to account for this new change.

  You can find a link to a template of the GSOT artifact at www.chaostoconcept.com/workshop/GSOT.

- **Personas or "user segments" that are related to each objective.**
  Personas serve as a quick way to communicate some basic information about the user that you are trying to serve. When done well, personas are prioritized based on their relative impact on the business. Prioritization at this level helps product teams track and promote work that is most likely to positively impact the objectives.

  There are two key types of personas. The first type is backed by data and this is usually simply referred to as a persona. The second type is not backed by data. This type of persona is called a proto-persona and is created using anecdotal information gathered from the stakeholders. The first type, and most valuable to your organization, is the research-backed persona. These personas are built using data that your team has gathered from usage analytics, input from direct conversations with customers, and demographic information from the sales and marketing team. The proto-persona can be valuable as well but only as a placeholder for a full persona. If you don't have the data it's still better to document your team's understanding of your users so that you can begin the process of validating your understanding and identifying areas where

Site Redesign GSOT Document
Version: 1.0
Prepared by: Kevin Braun
12/6/2013

Goals (The business outcome)	Strategies	Objectives	Tactics
Increase top-line (revenue) by X% by Y Time	Launch a newly designed Website (using leading practices in UX and front-end development) to support the major marketing push of acquiring new clients	Generate X number of qualified new leads within the first Y number of months after launch	SEO to drive organic traffic
			Paid search to drive targeted traffic
			Lite design with scrolling
			Info graphics — is this the right terminology?
			Potential use of video
			Responsive design for tablet and mobile use
		Content lift that provides prospective clients clear messages on services (methods of measuring success - time on site, page views, conversion)	Develop content for Ecommerce and content management solutions – CMX
			Develop content for Managed Care
			Develop content for infrastructure
			Clear calls to action
		Use Sitecore 7 to showcase the work	Certify staff on Sitecore 7
Improve bottom-line (operational efficiency)	Create and Follow SDLC lite 'UX design' process	Be able to complete the requirements phase of a site redesign project within X number of weeks	Review current SDLC and make recommendations for streamlining

Figure 1.4: A GSOT document serves as the core document in the constitution for your project and everyone on the team should have access to it so they can refer to it when questions arise.

your team's assumptions are incorrect. The UX process isn't a one-time exercise, so iteration on your personas shouldn't be considered a problem. UX is nothing if not a continuous iterative process.

- **Scenarios that are related to each persona.**
  Scenarios are very short stories that communicate what the persona is trying to accomplish. Scenarios also serve the purpose of providing context for use cases (more on those shortly) and should be directly related to both a persona and at least one objective.

  An example scenario might be something like "Average Dad Brad wants to buy a birthday gift for his son." Notice how short that is. There is no need for a lengthy, overly detailed description that is filled with information that will distract from what really needs to be focused on. In this case we know what persona it serves and that it is related to the objective of purchasing a gift.

  These can also be written as user stories if you are working in a Agile environment. It is pretty simple to translate this scenario into a user story. *As an* average dad *I would like to* be able to purchase a birthday gift for my son *so that* I will not be late giving him a gift and he will get what he asked me for.

If your team walks out of the workshop having consensus on those key outcomes, you have succeeded at this stage of the process. With that done, you are ready to move on to documenting the current status and performance of the systems you are working to improve with this project.

State of the Union

Where does your system stand in relation to UX industry standard heuristics as well as when compared to your competition?

Heuristic Evaluations

Heuristics can be thought of as a way of assessing how your product measures up to a set of UX industry standards. The most widely used set of heuristics was created by Jacob Nielsen. You can find an introductory article along with more in-depth information on the Nielsen Norman Group website at:

www.nngroup.com/articles/ten-usability-heuristics

I'll be referencing other information from the Nielsen Norman Group among others throughout this book. In most cases I'll share a link to the original work because each link will also serve as a great resource for further reading, and because I wouldn't want anyone to think these ideas originated with me. I've been on a 20+ year journey learning from many sources and my hope is that you'll find value in accessing those sources directly yourself.

A quick overview of Nielsen's heuristics includes the following 10 key elements to consider:

- **Visibility of system status**

  This has been achieved if users are easily able to understand where they are in the system, where they can go, and where they have been. Another element of this has to do with the status of system processes, such as loading a document, saving your work, etc. In general, if users find themselves lost in the system or wondering what is currently happening with the system, this criterion should be noted as needing more attention from your team.

- **Match between system and the real world**

  Systems that fail to meet this criterion usually do so because their interface matches the programmatic structure of the system rather than the user expectations (or mental model) of how it should work. An example of this could be a database of items in a grocery store. The items in the grocery store might logically be listed in the database in alphabetical order. This would make perfect sense from a software development point of view, but if we then organized the items in the grocery store using the same logic, a shopper could be standing in an aisle that included paper towels, puppy food, and petunias. Users have come to expect that paper towels would be in an aisle with other paper products like toilet paper and that petunias would be in the florist area of the store, so this would indicate a poor match between the system and the real world.

- **User control and freedom**

  In general, a great experience includes being able to explore a system without worrying that you are going to break something or have to spend a bunch of time recovering from a mistake. Users often encounter issues related to this criterion when they find themselves in the situation of needing to ask someone for help because they have taken an action that either resulted in something they don't understand or that was undesirable without knowing how to fix it. Providing a clear way to understand what will happen when an action is taken along with quick methods to undo unwanted actions will help to resolve most issues represented in this criterion.

- **Consistency and standards**

  You'll read multiple times in this book that a user's experience is greatly impacted by their ability to scan, read, and comprehend the content within the system. This criterion impacts a user's ability to understand what is on any given page more than almost anything else. Consistent header styles allow the user to understand where to find that information from page to page without having to consciously think about it. Consistency and standards help users know what to expect when moving through the system, and that confidence allows them to focus more of their attention on completing their tasks.

- **Error prevention**

  The only thing better than helping users quickly recover from their mistakes is to help them never make a mistake in the first place. One of the best ways to help users avoid errors is to ensure that you provide clear instructions, content, and messaging written using terms that are familiar to the user.

- **Recognition rather than recall**

  I often hear product owners say, "we'll make sure we provide training for users on that." Whenever I hear that I think of this criterion because in a perfect system, users would be able to recognize exactly how each element of the system works without training. That's obviously not always practical for many reasons but ensuring that your system is as intuitive as possible will improve engagement and retention and reduce training-related costs.

- **Flexibility and efficiency of use**

  The interface that is the easiest for a beginner to understand will often not be the most efficient interface for an expert user. I make sure to consider this when kicking off a project. If I'm working on a website that users won't use very often, I'll lean toward making it as easy to understand as possible. This would include using text labels that take up more room than icons, for example, so that users don't have to guess what will happen when they click.

  If I'm working on software that will be used in a busy call center, I'll make sure the interface and interactions are as efficient as possible. In some cases that might mean that I use icons instead of buttons with full labels because I can fit more icons on the screen in the same amount of space. In this case new users might not know what to do and potentially make mistakes, but expert users who use the system all day every day as part of their work will appreciate being able to get as much done as possible with the fewest interactions and in the smallest amount of time.

  Those examples are on the extreme ends of the spectrum, and for this criterion to truly be met a hybrid approach should be used that provides an interface that is explanatory and intuitive for new users while simultaneously including shortcuts and preference settings for expert users so they are not slowed down by the interface.

- **Aesthetic and minimalist design**

  Aesthetics are difficult to quantify because everyone has different taste. To meet the first part of this criterion I look for what I call *thematic appropriateness* in the interface. One example of this is a website that sells baby clothing. Pastel colors, handwritten gestural text in hero images, and baby animal imagery (chicks, ducklings, baby lambs) could all be appropriate thematic choices. There are countless other choices that could be made that would also be appropriate, so when I'm evaluating this, I'm usually looking for elements of the interface that clearly contradict the branding, concept, or theme of the system. I usually encounter issues with the aesthetic part of this criterion in off-brand color choices or the use of buttons and icons that don't support the overall messaging of the system.

  Development frameworks including Bootstrap can have a negative impact on the thematic appropriateness of a website because they make it so easy to get from 0% to

80% done with the design that many teams stop there. Not considering that last 20% can dilute your brand and make a bad impression on customers.

The minimalist design part of this criterion ties in nicely with Edward Tufte's precept about "data to ink." Tufte states that the best data visualizations include only the ink (or pixels) required to communicate the meaning of the data. Over the course of the last decade almost all major operating systems including Microsoft Windows, macOS, iOS, and Android have transitioned a design style called "flat design." The foundation of flat design is the idea that the interface should only comprise the elements required to communicate the meaning of the content and facilitate the interactions needed for users to complete their tasks.

This concept can be taken too far. If designers oversimplify interface elements in an attempt to satisfy the minimalist design criterion, they risk making interactions undiscoverable by removing all affordances.

- **Help users recognize, diagnose, and recover from errors**

  If you have ever filled out an online form, you have likely encountered systems that fail at meeting this criterion. When a form is submitted with errors the system should present the user with notifications about what is wrong, where it is wrong, and ideally with instructions that explain how to fix the issues. It's best to message users in context so they can easily make the connection between the error message and the specific item that needs to be fixed.

- **Help and documentation**

  Even in the best designed systems users will need documentation to help them learn what features are available and how they work. Users will also need help from time to time. Documentation needs to be comprehensive and easily accessed. Help is best when provided in context with a strong focus on solutions for the immediate need along with information on how to avoid errors in the future.

  A heuristic evaluation isn't a replacement for usability testing with representative users, but it is still important because it helps to provide an overview of issues that need to be addressed and can help your team make progress while awaiting qualitative information from usability testing sessions.

  Figure 1.5 shows what a heuristic evaluation might look like. You can find a link to a heuristic evaluation template at www.chaostoconcept.com/heurisitcs.

Expert Reviews

Heuristic evaluations and expert reviews go hand in hand. I'll often perform an expert review before working on the heuristic evaluation so I can become familiar with a system and with the basic user flows that are key to the system's success. This process helps me get my head in the game for kicking off usability testing, for completing a heuristic evaluation, or simply to be able to discuss viable next steps with a new client. Whatever the purpose, this is usually my first step when kicking off a new project.

[Client Name] Heuristic Evaluation – **[Date]**

#	Heuristic	Yes, No, N/A	Severity	Comments	Location
1000	**Visibility of System Status**				
1001	Does every display begin with a title or header that describes screen contents?	Yes	1		
1002	Is there a consistent icon design scheme and stylistic treatment across the system?	No	2		
1003	Is a single, selected icon clearly visible when surrounded by unselected icons?	N/A	3		
1004	Do menu instructions, prompts, and error messages appear in the same place(s) on each menu?				
1005	In multipage data entry screens, is each page labeled to show its relation to others?				
1006	If over-type and insert mode are both available, is there a visible indication of which one the user is in?				
1007	If pop-up windows are used to display error messages, do they allow the user to see the field in error?				
1008	Is there some form of system feedback for every operator action?				
1009	After the user completes an action (or group of actions), does the feedback indicate that the next group of actions can be started?				
1010	Is there visual feedback in menus or dialog boxes about which choices are selectable?				
1011	Is there visual feedback in menus or dialog boxes about which choice the cursor is on now?				
1012	If multiple options can be selected in a menu or dialog box, is there visual feedback about which options are already selected?				
1013	Is there visual feedback when objects are selected or moved?				
1014	Is the current status of an icon clearly indicated?				
1015	Is there feedback when function keys are pressed?				
1016	If there are observable delays (greater than fifteen seconds) in the system's response time, is the user kept informed of the system's progress?				
1017	Are response times appropriate to the task?				
1018	Typing, cursor motion, mouse selection: 50-150 milliseconds				
1019	Simple, frequent tasks: less than 1 second				
1020	Common tasks: 2-4 seconds				
1021	Complex tasks: 8-12 seconds				
1022	Are response times appropriate to the user's cognitive processing?				
1023	Continuity of thinking is required and information must be remembered throughout several responses: less than two seconds.				
1024	High levels of concentration aren't necessary and remembering information is not required: two to fifteen seconds.				
1025	Is the menu-naming terminology consistent with the user's task domain?				
1026	Does the system provide visibility: that is, by looking, can the user tell the state of the system and the alternatives for action?				
1027	Do GUI menus make obvious which item has been selected?				
1028	Do GUI menus make obvious whether deselection is possible?				
1029	If users must navigate between multiple screens, does the system use context labels, menu maps, and place markers as navigational aids?				
2000	**Match Between System and the Real World**				
2001	Are icons concrete and familiar?				
2002	Are menu choices ordered in the most logical way, given the user, the item names, and the task variables?				

Figure 1.5: A heuristic evaluation helps customers see exactly where their issues are and where their system stands against a set of industry standard measures.

To successfully complete an expert review, you need to have a solid understanding of what users are trying to achieve when using the system. Next, you should do the research necessary to understand what user expectations are based on industry leaders in the space along with researching best practices for each of the key interactions that make up the user journeys. This gets easier with time, but even very experienced professionals should still take the time to verify that there haven't been advancements in trends or approaches that they are not aware of.

With that foundation in place, I begin the process of walking through each step in each use case and document any issues I find that are likely to impact a user along the way. Oftentimes the issues I find are related to the system not providing enough context or information for the user to be able to make an informed decision about how to proceed. Other issues I frequently encounter include visual hierarchies that are hard to scan, read, or comprehend along with interactions that do not facilitate an efficient experience for the user.

An example of how I might document issues I find while performing an expert review is shown in Figure 1.6. This also illustrates something else that is very important to remember: Don't always do what Apple, Google, or Amazon do without question. They are all amazing teams with a lot more design talent than I personally possess, but that doesn't mean everything they do is right. The figure is an example from the very first page of Apple's Human Interface Guidelines. I've highlighted their guidelines, and where

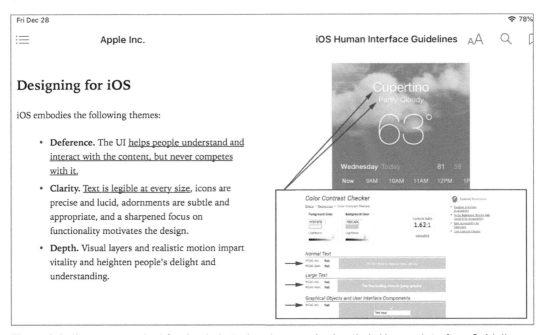

Figure 1.6: I've never worked for Apple but when I was reviewing their Human Interface Guidelines, I was shocked to find this issue on the very first page.

their example of the right way to do it fails basic accessibility testing. When I find issues like this, I document them using a similar format so I can share them with my clients to help in the prioritization process.

The concept of expectancy is very important when trying to understand what users will find easy to use. Oftentimes a user's repeated interactions with Apple, Amazon, or Google products will lead them to expect your system to function like theirs do. It's very important to keep this in mind and leverage it where possible to avoid re-creating the wheel. I provided this example to make it clear that all of us should also use our critical thinking skills and not simply follow the leaders blindly.

When I find issues in an expert review, I add them to a spreadsheet that I've created (see Figure 1.7) to track problems and help facilitate the discussions on how to resolve them. It's a fairly simple sheet that helps to keep track of where the issue happened, a brief description of the issue and how to repeat it, a link to an annotated screenshot, potential resolutions, projected impact, and perceived difficulty to resolve. This is my process and it's always evolving. I offer this version to you as a starting point for creating your own.

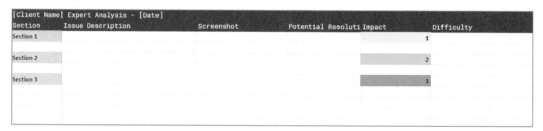

Figure 1.7: Like the heuristic evaluation, an expert review document like this can help a team work together on a review and allows customers to easily see and track their issues.

You can find a link to an expert review template at www.chaostoconcept.com/expert-reviews.

Competitive Analysis

Other helpful information can be gathered by performing a competitive analysis. Understanding how your solution is functioning in relation to your competition consists of the four key elements I'll discuss here. Most companies cannot accurately report on all four, so don't get discouraged if you start off with only a fraction of what is recommended. Even the preamble to the Constitution of the United States recognizes that nothing starts off perfectly, and also acknowledges that perfection may not be possible by stating ". . . in order to form a *more* perfect union." No matter what you are building, take comfort in knowing that no part of the UX process is a one-time fix. Iteration based on data creates a solid foundation and sets your team up with a repeatable process for continuous improvement.

The key elements of a competitive analysis include establishing a strong understanding of the Market Share, Product Perception, Feature Matrix, and Value.

Market Share

The formula to calculate your market share is pretty simple:

Market share = Your total revenues divided by the industry's total sales during a fixed period

To determine what an industry's value is it will be easiest to review reports put out by industry organizations or look at the annual reports of some of the biggest players in the industry.

If your team can accurately understand market share and penetration, you'll be able to make strategic shifts in how your business is run. Early in the game acquisition is essential, while later in your product's life cycle, hopefully you'll be able to shift to a more defensive retention focus. Either way the first step is to gather the information required to understand your position. The sales and marketing teams will likely be your best source of this info. If you are working at a small startup, the founders are your best bet and hopefully you're already working very closely with them.

Product Perception

Your team can track brand perception in a number of different ways. The methods I've seen most frequently used within product design teams are the Net Promoter Score and Google's HEART framework.

The Net Promoter Score (NPS) is a method used by companies around the world to gauge the relative happiness of their customers on a scale from 0 to 10. You are not likely to be able to get hold of your competitors' NPS scores, but you can get some general industry benchmarks.

Retently publishes a set of benchmarks that can be viewed on their site at: www.retently .com/blog/good-net-promoter-score.

To gather the data for your NPS, participants are asked, "On a scale of 0 to 10, how likely are you to recommend this company's product or service to a friend or colleague?"

0–6. Participants who rate your product between 0 and 6 are called *detractors* in this system. Detractors are not very happy with your product and they won't likely purchase again or recommend your product.

7–8. Participants who rate your product 7 or 8 are considered to be *passive*. Passive participants are not actively upset with your product but are not overly satisfied with it either. These participants are likely to switch to another product, and if they recommend your product it will likely be with caveats.

9–10. Participants who rate your product 9 or 10 are labeled *promoters*. These participants are happy with your product and are likely to unconditionally recommend it.

This question is often asked at the end of a survey while gathering other info. Once you have gathered your scores, you'll need to calculate them using the following formula:

$$NPS = \% \text{ of promoters} - \% \text{ of detractors}$$

To calculate that you'll first need to know the % that were promoters by using the following formula:

$$\% \text{ of promoters} = \# \text{ of promoters} / \# \text{ of respondents}$$

To calculate the % of detractors you would need to use the following formula:

$$\% \text{ of detractors} = \# \text{ of detractors} / \# \text{ of respondents}$$

Once you have that done, you can go back and plug the numbers into the NPS score formula and perform the final calculation.

Now that you see how it works, it is important to know that you don't need to calculate it the hard way. You can find several online calculators, including this one from Survey-Monkey: www.surveymonkey.com/mp/nps-calculator.

Google's HEART Framework

In this context, HEART stands for Happiness, Engagement, Adoption, Retention, and Task Success (see Figure 1.8). This is one of Google's tools for measuring how their solutions are performing. This approach combines some of the other methods we have reviewed with new methods, resulting in a comprehensive framework. This is another one of those systems that could be difficult to set up within your organization, but it can be worth it if you have a team that is committed to monitoring and maintaining it. In the organization I was working at when I was introduced to this method, it was set up with a dashboard for various teams to monitor. I believe members of the executive team were very excited by this dashboard because it was the first time they could actually see on one page a relatively real-time view of how their system was performing. There were flaws in our execution, and keeping the data current and complete proved to be too much of a challenge for the team over time, but what I saw while it was running was enough to convince me of the value.

What I like about this framework is how closely it ties to the overall approach outlined in this book. There is a strong focus on defined goals and measuring your progress, so adapting this framework is pretty straightforward.

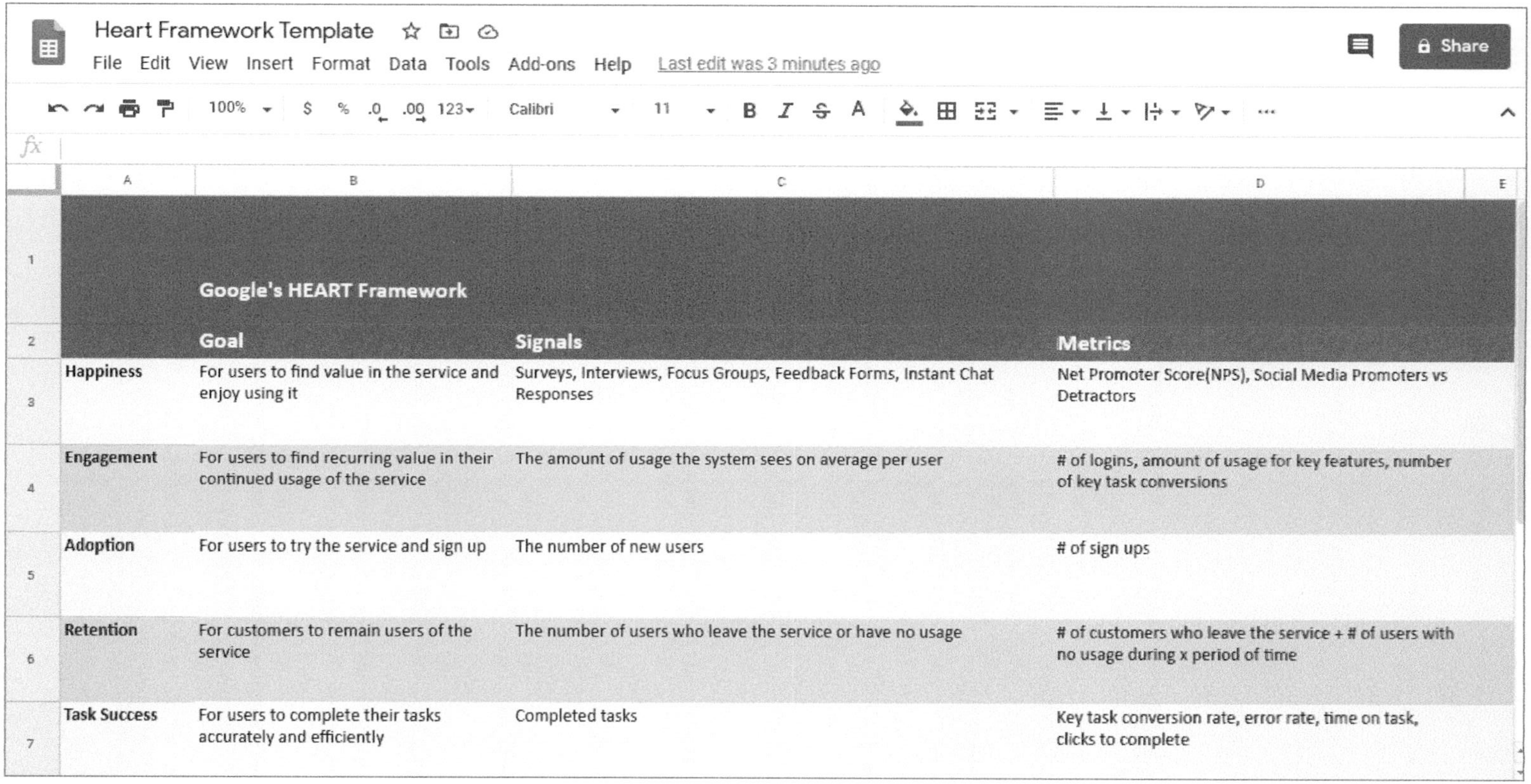

Heart Framework Template

File Edit View Insert Format Data Tools Add-ons Help   Last edit was 3 minutes ago

Google's HEART Framework

	Goal	Signals	Metrics
Happiness	For users to find value in the service and enjoy using it	Surveys, Interviews, Focus Groups, Feedback Forms, Instant Chat Responses	Net Promoter Score(NPS), Social Media Promoters vs Detractors
Engagement	For users to find recurring value in their continued usage of the service	The amount of usage the system sees on average per user	# of logins, amount of usage for key features, number of key task conversions
Adoption	For users to try the service and sign up	The number of new users	# of sign ups
Retention	For customers to remain users of the service	The number of users who leave the service or have no usage	# of customers who leave the service + # of users with no usage during x period of time
Task Success	For users to complete their tasks accurately and efficiently	Completed tasks	Key task conversion rate, error rate, time on task, clicks to complete

Figure 1.8: The HEART Framework by Google Ventures is a helpful way to track your team's progress and communicate issues and opportunities with executive teams.

Similar to a lot of what you read in this book, any effort in the right direction is better than no effort. If your team can only manage to accurately and consistently report on a small piece of the information that makes up the HEART framework, you are still better off than if you don't measure any of it. Adoption is an easy place to start, followed by engagement and retention. Every situation is different, so I'm going to summarize all of them and provide a direct link to Google's info on the subject so you can dig deeper if you are interested.

Happiness

You can measure happiness in a few different ways. You can ask questions about satisfaction via a survey. You can rely on the Net Promoter Score that we discussed previously. You can also track social media and user forums to gather sentiment information. Whatever methods you choose, gathering information about happiness will allow you to better understand the impact of issues you may uncover elsewhere. If you have a technical issue and your happiness indicators don't change all that much, then you can gauge future responses to that type of issue more accurately. If, on the other hand, something in your system that your team believed was trivial turns up on a user forum or Twitter as being a big problem and you see that other users are agreeing, sharing, or creating a hashtag about it, then you know your team needs to reprioritize that issue.

I've personally used the information gathered via the ForeSee pop-up feedback prompt to identify and raise issues for prioritization, so I know that direct information about customer sentiment can be very helpful.

Engagement

Engagement is an interesting thing to track. If you ask most product owners today, you'll likely hear that they want their product to be addictive. What this usually means is that they want users to engage with their product every day and ideally multiple times a day.

That actually doesn't always make much sense. If a user is an executive who is checking in on how the operations are going across the country, she might not really need to do that every day. It's possible that checking in at this level twice a week might make more sense for her. It's also possible that 30 seconds of reviewing a dashboard twice a week under normal circumstances represents a wonderful user experience for the executive in question.

I understand that your business wants to be able to illustrate strong engagement, but I don't recommend forcing the issue. If you have a compelling user need that you can address on a daily basis, by all means work toward that. If not, stating daily usage as a goal can distract from goals that could be achieved and can discourage your teams by needlessly directing them to work on something that is likely unattainable.

My suggestion is to base your initial engagement goals on anticipated user needs and then work from there to add value that might drive more engagement over time.

Adoption

As I mentioned before, adoption should be relatively simple to monitor. You'll be looking to track new signups, new trials, etc., as a way of understanding how many new customers you have in the system week to week, month over month, and year over year. Keeping track of adoption is a great indicator of how well your product is fitting within your market.

Retention

This is all about keeping the users you already have because they are usually the most valuable to your organization. This often gets measured on a spectrum. You might report on the number of users who log in daily as part of engagement and use that same method to report on those users who have logged in at least once in the past month as being retained. However your business decides to measure it, retention is all about tracking your success at keeping users and is an essential part of understanding how changes to your offerings are impacting the user experience.

Task Success

Task success broadly relates to what most people think of as a conversion. Conversions are thought of as the end goal of a user's interactions with a system. An example of a conversion might be a completed checkout on an ecommerce site. Another example would be a contact form submission on a marketing site. Defining your key tasks and what the outcome should be is an essential part of measuring and improving on your user experience.

To read a lot more about Google's HEART framework, visit this URL:

ai.google/research/pubs/pub36299

Feature Matrix

Another tool that is essential to understanding how your product or service compares with the competition is a feature comparison matrix. This is usually a simple spreadsheet that starts off with a comprehensive list of features offered in the market in one column on the far left and then a list including your product and all of your competitors each in their own cell in the top row of the spreadsheet. Below each product name is usually a check for each feature that is offered in that product. If a feature isn't offered, that cell is left empty. Once you have completed the matrix, it is very easy to see how all the products in the market relate to one another in terms of features as shown in Figure 1.9.

A more complex version of this takes into account the relative priority each feature has in relation to your most valuable user's scenarios. To calculate this, you first need to rank your personas by their relative value to your organization. This is most often tied to revenue, but for some companies influencers are more important early on because they are more focused on attracting and building audience, etc. Either way it's important to rank your personas so that you can make design decisions based on their value. We'll discuss creating personas and prioritizing them in detail later in the book, but for the sake of this conversation just know that it's important to have them because they provide a context for understanding your position in the market.

Once you have the personas ranked, you'll need to have a list of the features that are important to your most valuable users. You can gather that list of features by itemizing what features are required to complete each scenario that is associated with that persona.

If your most important users need a way to find a ride on demand, such as when using an app like Uber, they will need at least the following features to satisfy that scenario:

1. Geolocation so the app knows where to send the car for the pickup
2. An account associated with payment information
3. The ability for users to enter a start and ending location
4. A time and cost estimate
5. A ride type selector
6. A confirmation and pickup time estimation

Once you have that information, you can assign a higher value to the features on the list so that when you complete your matrix you'll have a clearer picture of how your solution compares to your competition when it comes to what your most valuable users need.

You can find a link to a feature matrix template at www.chaostoconcept.com/feature-matrix.

Value

In my experience, value is very rarely calculated because many think that it's too subjective or inaccurate. I believe this is going to be an essential metric as UX and

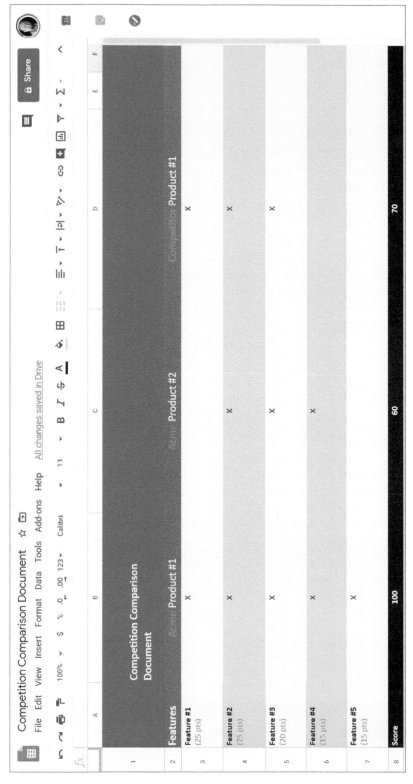

Features	Acme Product #1	Acme Product #2	Competitor Product #1
Feature #1 (25 pts)	X		X
Feature #2 (25 pts)	X	X	X
Feature #3 (20 pts)	X	X	X
Feature #4 (15 pts)	X	X	
Feature #5 (15 pts)	X		
Score	100	60	70

Figure 1.9: A feature matrix is a great way to document how your product compares to others in the market. It is also a great way to visualize the specifics of what makes the market leaders stand out.

product teams mature. In hopes of spearheading the conversation on this topic, I offer the following formula:

I'm about to geek out here for a bit and what I'm about to describe isn't established best practice so if you aren't interested in learning about this at the moment, skip ahead to page 28.

Value = The prioritized and weighted product features divided by the Normalized Price (yearly, monthly, etc.) across the market

This sounds more complicated than it really is. If you completed the advanced feature matrix reviewed previously, you already have the prioritized and weighted features. The normalized price is calculated by looking at all the competition's pricing models and converting each so that they are all being measured in the same way.

If your product offers only a monthly subscription, you would start off by saying that the normalized price is $15.00 per month.

If Competitor A has a monthly and yearly pricing plan, you would use the one that adds upto the cheapest monthly payment. For this example, we will say that their price is $20.00 per month.

If Competitor B offers a one-time purchase price, we'll assume a lifetime for this product to be four years before a major upgrade that requires another payment. Let's say that their one-time price is $199.00. You would then divide that by 48 months and get a normalized price of $4.14 a month. Obviously this price would seem to be a big advantage but a lump sum payment of $199.00 can be a substantial barrier to entry, especially for a consumer product, so that needs to be factored in.

This is where you'll likely need to make some adjustments based on the relative price points, but for this example I would say any product with a one-time price greater than $25.00 and less than $50.00 would get a $5.00 a month penalty with an additional $5.00 a month penalty added for each $50.00 above that. For this example, the $199.00 one-time price would normalize to $4.14 a month and would receive a penalty of $15.00 a month, making the total adjusted monthly cost $19.14 per month.

The adjusted price breakdown looks like this:

$199.00 / 48 = $4.14

One-time price between $25.00 and $50.00 = $5.00 penalty

One-time price additional penalty for the next $50.00 = an additional $5.00 penalty

One-time price additional penalty for the next $50.00 = an additional $5.00 penalty

Since $199.00 is less than $200.00 we stop there and add the penalty to the normalized price and end up with the $19.14 mentioned previously.

With this calculation done, our market normalized price range is:

Your product: $15.00 per month

Competitor A: $20.00 per month

Competitor B: $19.14 per month

Now that we have the normalized prices, we need the values for the prioritized and weighted features. As mentioned previously, in the advanced feature matrix process we prioritize and weight our features by defining those features that are most important to our most valuable personas or user segments. We'll discuss creating personas and prioritizing them in detail later in the book, but for the sake of this conversation just know that it's important to have them because they provide a context for understanding the value of various features.

For this example, let's say we added up the feature value points for your product and found that it scored 17. Each feature your product has is worth 1 point. Your product offers a total of 12 of the 16 features available in your market so you start off with 12 points. Five of those features are essential to your most valuable users, so each of those gets an extra point.

With the weighted features accounted for, those 5 features add up to 10 points.

The remaining 7 standard features add up to 7 points.

Adding these together we end up with a total of 17 feature points for your product.

Let's assume we completed the same process for the other two products and ended up with 20 feature points for Competitor A and 12 feature points for Competitor B.

With all that done, we are ready to plug the numbers into the value formula to better understand our product's relative value. The higher the value index, the better.

Your Product Value:
    17 / 15.00 = 1.13

Competitor A's Product Value:
    20 / 20.00 = 1.00

Competitor B's Product Value:
    12 / 19.14 = .062

I believe this type of value scoring is important because it provides a clear way to understand your position in the market and also establishes a clear link between price and functionality in relation to what your most valuable customers need.

Benchmarking, KPIs, and OKRs

Benchmarking, internal and external, is pretty simple. It is also essential to the iterative design process because it is the foundation for how we'll track our progress. In order to establish a benchmark, you'll be tracking how your competition compares to your product in relation to very specific conversion goals.

Documenting the number of clicks a user must initiate to complete the checkout process in an ecommerce site is a great example of a competitive benchmark. It would be relatively easy to visit each of your competitors, add a product to the cart, and then start counting the number of clicks it takes to complete that checkout. You would then do the same thing with your other competitor sites. Once you have all those clicks to complete benchmark numbers you can compare them to your own product to understand and track your relative performance. There are other ways to track this sort of thing, such as measuring the time it takes a user to complete a task or measuring the number of mistakes a user makes while completing a use case.

KPIs (Key Performance Indicators)

Monitoring the number of successful task completions (conversion rate) or the number of customers who added at least one item to the cart (micro conversion) is an example of tracking your KPIs. For non-ecommerce systems, you could track the end state of any meaningful workflow as a conversion along with important substeps in a workflow as micro conversion.

Tracking all the micro conversion and the final conversion in a single workflow can be thought of as a *conversion funnel*. All this means is that you are tracking each step in a workflow and monitoring the number of users who successfully complete each step. Because these are usually linear processes, the fall off rate (number of users who drop out of the process at any given step) usually resembles a funnel if you were to illustrate it. To picture this, imagine that you have 100 users visit your site (the wide end of the funnel) and that 50 of them visited a product page. In this case the product page visit micro conversion rate would be 50%. Now imagine that of those 50 product page visits 10 of those users added a product to their cart. That would mean you have a 10% add to cart micro conversion rate. Finally, imagine that 1 of those 10 that added a product to the cart went on to finish the checkout process. That would mean that your overall conversion rate is 1% and that represents the narrow end of the funnel as seen in Figure 1.10.

Tracking these types of indicators will help your team understand the overall performance of your system and will also provide vision into whether the changes you are making along the way are helping or hurting your business. This is very important because your iterations will rely on an accurate flow or performance data to provide direction.

Figure 1.10: Conversion funnels are an industry-standard way of visualizing how well your system is moving users through the process.

OKRs (Objectives and Key Results)

Another term you will hear is OKR, or Objectives and Key Results. This process is essentially the same as what I described when introducing Goals, Strategies, Objectives, and Tactics. The idea is to define your objectives and make sure you have a way of measuring success or failure. One addition that I'll make based on the following article from Google Ventures (`library.gv.com/how-google-sets-goals-okrs-a1f69b0b72c7`) is that there is a sweet spot in your success rate. If you are 60% to 70% successful, you're doing great. That means that you have moved the needle in the right direction and that your objectives were sufficiently challenging. If you are always scoring 90% to 100% you can be happy about the progress, but it also likely indicates that your objectives aren't ambitious enough. This isn't a new system, but in many ways it feels like it is just now starting to gain widespread acceptance.

MAKE IT USABLE

"Design is a funny word. Some people think design means how it looks. But of course, if you dig deeper, it's really how it **works**."

—Steve Jobs

Who Are We Designing This For?— Personas/User Segments

The first principle of the Agile Manifesto is "Our highest priority is to satisfy the customer through early and continuous delivery of valuable software." It is very hard to deliver valuable software if you don't know who you are developing it for and what they will find valuable.

When you left off from your workshop you should have ended up with some objectives. Those Objectives and Key Results (OKRs), are important to the process for a number of reasons, but at the moment they are important because they serve as a foundation for the next step.

If you are already convinced of the need to understand your users and use that understanding to drive your design process, you can skip ahead to page 34. If, on the other hand, you want to read my thoughts on one of the biggest issues impacting the user experience industry, continue reading right from here.

It's time to put the U in UX. It's sad, but this step is often overlooked and skipped altogether. I realize people want to be nice and flexible and not hurt anyone's feelings by excluding some people from being able to say they are user experience designers, but that isn't helping anyone, and it is, in fact, hurting many businesses. I'm stating here unequivocally that if your process doesn't include defining your users, conducting research with participants that represent your target demographic, and using what you learn from that research to drive the decisions in your design process, then you *are not* conducting user-centered design.

This is a very important concept to understand because most graphic design programs at colleges and universities do not include anything about defining users, doing research, or distilling the information gathered from users into requirements. Most also don't teach anything about interaction design, either. These are just a few pieces of the process that are missing, but they are essential. For many businesses that means the person they are relying on to design their user experience hasn't been trained to do it. The business ends up disappointed in the results and blaming the designer. In many cases, designers blame themselves as well. It's all unfair and avoidable.

For developers, it is the opposite. It is pretty common to hear business owners apologize for their terrible UX by saying that they didn't have anyone on staff who was responsible for it, so it was left to the developers. Most don't expect developers to do a good job with the UX of their product because it is understood that they were never trained to do that work. That same understanding needs to be passed along to most graphic designers and they then need to be supported with training opportunities or additional staff who will take on the areas they are not experts in.

It might be tempting to read this and think that you don't need graphic designers, and that you could skip them altogether and just get a user experience designer. That may be true, but most likely isn't. The first problem with that approach is that there are very few people trained and experienced in the broad-ranging skill set that makes up modern user experience design. If you do find someone with all those skills and some real-world experience applying them, expect to pay them at least $150K even in the smallest markets as of mid-2019. Trust me, finding and hiring these people isn't easy. It's also not always the best approach.

If you have one of those rare people on your team, you'll run into the next problem: they are still human. Their humanity will most likely become an issue for your business when you realize that they aren't like computers and very often their work will be single-threaded. That means that they'll be focused on workshops and gathering requirements or they'll be focused on research and analysis or they'll be neck-deep in designing user flows and interactions, but you'll soon discover that one person can't do all these things at the same time and therefore will become a bottleneck for your team.

This is where hiring a team of T-shaped designers shines. I first read about T-shaped designers in Robert Hoekman's book, *Experience Required*. This concept was something I was very aware of but not something I had given a name, and I'm very glad Hoekman did because it helps me communicate this idea with my students and customers. T-shaped designers are those that have a broad set of skills that represent the top horizontal line of the T and they also go deep into at least one of those skills. That depth represents the vertical line in the T. These people working as a team can move fluidly between the various parts of the holistic UX process and support each other and the business at the same time. They can help ramp up your graphic designers in areas where they need more exposure, while the graphic designers help them learn more about how type, color, composition, visual hierarchy, etc., all play an essential part in creating a great experience that also represents the company's brand.

Graphic designers and developers both have a tremendous impact on the final experience that your customers will use every day, so my recommendation is to include user-centered design training for those who want it. There are a few reputable sources that can provide training opportunities in small chunks that are manageable while working a full-time job. I recommend the Interaction Design Foundation (www.interaction-design.org) because their courses have some of the best materials available and the cost is pretty inexpensive.

If you can't support paying for the training, get some copies of the books I recommend throughout this book and offer them up to those who are interested. If no one on your team steps forward as being interested, you have a bigger problem. If too many people step forward, you should be thrilled. That means they are engaged and actively want to be a part of making your product better. Investing in these employees is a good business decision. I've created a list of great UX books (www.brauninteractive.com/books) that cover various topics in detail. One cheap method of helping people learn is your local UX Meetup group. If you aren't already a member, Meetup.com is a great place to learn from local industry professionals for free or at a very low cost.

With all that being said, it's time to move on to defining our users. To do that, let's imagine that one of the objectives we are going to focus on is retention.

The actual objective might be worded something like this:

"Improve retention for our analytics product"
The key results or OKRs might look something like this:

- Reduce support calls (also improves operational efficiency)
- Improve our Net Promoter Score (NPS), currently at 32
- Create a customer advisory board and interview all new members to better understand their wants and needs

With those objectives in mind, the first step is to either create a persona that will be related to your objective or use an existing persona that you have already created that could be impacted by the objective.

Let's say that the first thing we want to work on is reducing support calls. That being the case, you would want to document the current amount of support calls in the last month and quarter. The time frame is a suggestion, but it is essential that you at least benchmark the current status of this metric.

Potential Blocker

If you don't have analytics set up, or don't have access to anyone who can provide this information to your team, you'll need to work to ensure that you set up a system to capture and report on this kind of information regularly. If it's not currently in place, add it to the list of things your team needs to address.
One place to start is Google Analytics:
support.google.com/analytics/answer/1008015?hl=en
It's free and will provide you with all the power you need to monitor your user experience.

To continue with this example, we'll say the number of support calls in the past month was 425 and in the past quarter, there were 1,500 calls. It is important to keep in mind that these numbers may be impacted by other factors outside of the user experience that come into play such as time of year, weather, political cycle, etc. The user experience is just one piece of the puzzle. An example of this might be if you were selling cars. Convertibles sell better in the spring/summer than they do in the fall/winter for obvious reasons. If you were trying to improve the user experience on a site that sells convertibles, the time of year would be a factor that you would consider when reviewing your other KPIs. Without digging too far into the details for this example, we'll round out our target number to 500 calls per month based on the quarterly (three-month) average of 1,500 calls.

After considering all of that, we now know that our goal is to have less than 500 calls per month following the release of the new solutions. Ideally, we would want to see a substantial drop in calls, but trending in the right direction is important as well.

To break down this problem further we'll want to find out what types of support calls are coming in. Usually interviewing the support personnel is the best way to learn more about how the calls break down into groups.

Imagine that after discussing the calls with three of your top support people, you find out that most of the calls fit into the groups shown in Table 2.1.

This is a frustratingly ambiguous real-world result. There is information here that can be acted on, but a full 35% is too vague to be actionable.

Even though this result isn't as clear cut as we might like, you can still make marked progress by addressing the product configuration this time around while conducting some more research to ensure that you have many of the "other" issues better defined for your next iteration.

Since product configuration is the big addressable issue at the moment, we'll create a new persona, the "Work from Home Dad," to begin defining the problem space.

The Work from Home Dad persona is different from other users. They have likely never used the system before and along with not being sure how to set the system up, they may also not understand what options are available.

If you do a web search on personas, you'll find that there are a lot of different ways designers document their users with personas. Some create beautifully designed artifacts and others create a Word document that includes only the text description of the user. Depending on the client, I do both of those and everything in between. I'll discuss how I choose what method is best later, but all include some essential elements in order for them to be useful.

Figure 2.1 is an example of a persona format developed by Jeff Volzer, a colleague of mine for many years who took over the UX Speakeasy in Burlington, Vermont, when I moved to California.

Table 2.1 Identified Issues

Issue	Rate of Occurrence
Account creation	5%
Login issues	3%
Billing issues	8%
Cancellation issues	4%
Issues with product configuration	45%
Other	35%

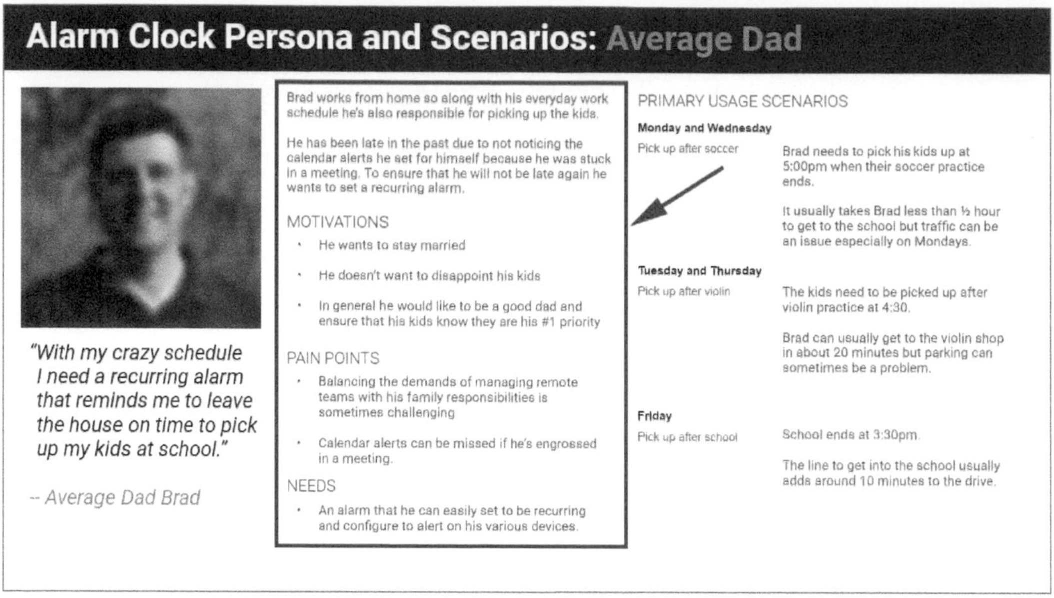

Alarm Clock Persona and Scenarios: Average Dad

Brad works from home so along with his everyday work schedule he's also responsible for picking up the kids.

He has been late in the past due to not noticing the calendar alerts he set for himself because he was stuck in a meeting. To ensure that he will not be late again he wants to set a recurring alarm.

MOTIVATIONS

- He wants to stay married
- He doesn't want to disappoint his kids
- In general he would like to be a good dad and ensure that his kids know they are his #1 priority

PAIN POINTS

- Balancing the demands of managing remote teams with his family responsibilities is sometimes challenging
- Calendar alerts can be missed if he's engrossed in a meeting.

NEEDS

- An alarm that he can easily set to be recurring and configure to alert on his various devices.

"With my crazy schedule I need a recurring alarm that reminds me to leave the house on time to pick up my kids at school."

-- Average Dad Brad

PRIMARY USAGE SCENARIOS

Monday and Wednesday
Pick up after soccer

Brad needs to pick his kids up at 5:00pm when their soccer practice ends.

It usually takes Brad less than ½ hour to get to the school but traffic can be an issue especially on Mondays.

Tuesday and Thursday
Pick up after violin

The kids need to be picked up after violin practice at 4:30.

Brad can usually get to the violin shop in about 20 minutes but parking can sometimes be a problem.

Friday
Pick up after school

School ends at 3:30pm.

The line to get into the school usually adds around 10 minutes to the drive.

Figure 2.1: Personas should be short and focus on real-world user goals, pain points, motivations, and needs.

The persona template in Figure 2.1 breaks down into the following key ingredients, but one key thing to keep in mind is that personas are living documents that change as your business iterates and pivots and as new information comes in from sales, research, and analytics. This is the main reason I recommend sticking with the format that is easiest for your teams to edit and collaborate on. A beautifully designed UX artifact that is stale and contains old, potentially misleading information is a dangerous thing. As with everything else in UX, keep it simple, keep it current, and keep iterating. The method you use to present them is less important than their content. Keeping that in mind, make sure yours include:

- **A one-paragraph general description of who this persona is.**
  People often go wrong writing this part by including irrelevant information. Oftentimes this irrelevant information comes in the form of age, education level, etc. These things could be essential but oftentimes they don't really have anything to do with how your users will interact with the system. The trick is to make sure that what you include is directly related to the system you are working to improve. If you are working on an application that is targeted toward kids, then the age will be important. If you are working on improving the checkout process on a site like amazon.com, age won't be as essential because it gets used by a wide age range. In the end, if you can explain why it's essential to include it, is probably fine to have it in your persona. If you can't, remove it.

- **Bullet points to cover the user's key motivations.**
  Document the high-level everyday realities that lead the user to be looking for a solution.

- **Bullet points to cover the user's key pain points.**
  List items to add some content so your team can understand the specific issues that this user is experiencing.

- **A bullet point or two to describe their needs.**
  State the problem this persona needs to have solved in the simplest terms. Don't include solutions here; just include the problem.

- **A user quote.**
  Ideally this will be a real user quote, but to start off it's fine to just summarize what the user needs. Once you have done some research and have real user quotes to pull from, update your persona based on all the new information.

Now that you have seen an example of a persona that is designed, it should be pretty easy to imagine how you would strip away the design elements and create an outline version of this in Word or a Google doc like Figure 2.2.

I. Developers and Operators/Owners

Example:
Paul is a developer who relies on the service to help him understand on a daily basis how well his site is operating. He's looking for comprehensive information about energy production relative to initial projections and available resources (i.e., irradiance.) If the site's performance is deviating from what was projected (or guaranteed), he needs tools that highlight why. If the underperformance is a service issue, he needs to be able to manage, track, and "close the loop" on the resulting service activity.

Goals:
1. Minimize downtime
2. Optimize service
3. Maximize ROI

Keys to happiness:
1. Timely data
2. Accurate data
3. Minimization of management workload
4. Local weather widget (such as Weatherbug) in UI when viewing current data
5. Access to wide area weather satellite images

KPIs, Reporting, or Visualization Requirements:
1. Site and portfolio performance (in summary and individually by MTD, QTD, YTD, and LTD totals, with 13-month graph, including environmental offsets)
2. Site and portfolio savings or revenue produced (in summary and individually (as above with 13-month graph)
3. Daily energy/revenue/environmental offsets

Figure 2.2: You don't need to be a designer to create personas. In many cases the less design the better, because they will be more likely to be kept current.

Usually, I'll try to define a draft of all the personas as part of a workshop with my clients. This helps me get a solid overview and allows the team to quickly remove those that substantially overlap with others to narrow our list to those that are most essential. In general, I've found that a small number of personas usually cover what's needed very well. Three to five is the number I most often end up with. If it's more than that, usually that's an indicator that the product we are working on might actually be two or more products. It's not a hard-and-fast rule, but something to consider as you are working on them.

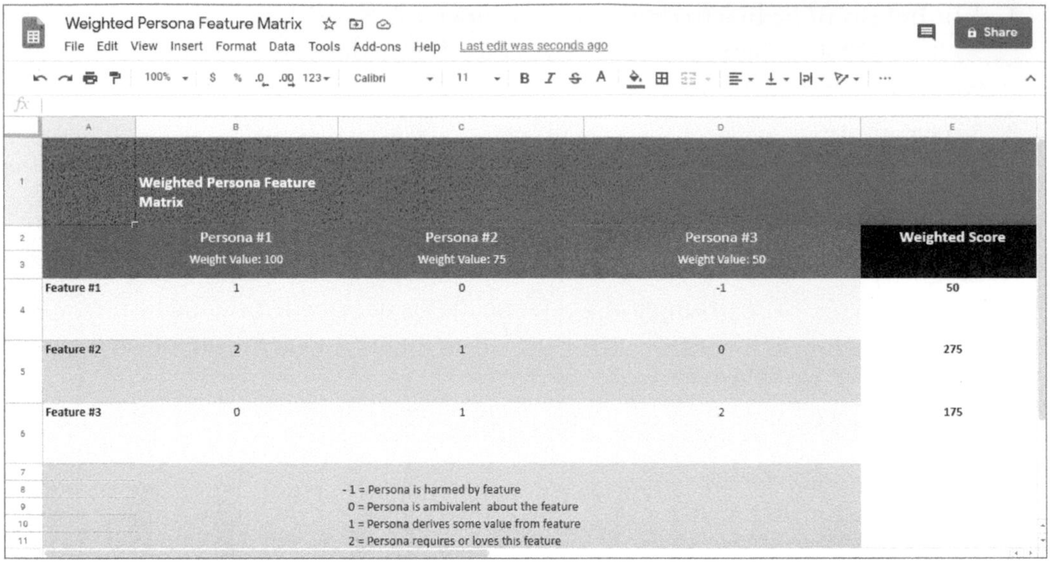

Figure 2.3: A persona value matrix is valuable because it clearly illustrates what personas are the highest priority for your business.

The last step you'll want to do is to prioritize the personas you end up with using a persona value matrix as illustrated in Figure 2.3. This means that you will need to determine each persona's relative value to the business. This is a very important step because later in the process you'll end up needing to make decisions about what features get built and what features get left in the backlog. When these situations arise, being able to associate the impact of adding a feature with a high-priority persona can help to keep it moving forward.

What Do They Need?—Scenarios

Whatever method you use to get there, after you have a solid understanding of who your users are it is time to document what those users need to do. This is the role of scenarios. You may hear these called "use cases" and in general, there is a lot of confusion about what both things are and how they differ. Use cases are another important part of the process that we'll discuss next, but for the moment I'll define scenarios as *what* a user needs to do and a use case as *how* the user will do it.

Figure 2.4 illustrates how I often break down what a user needs to do based on specific time frames. For some applications, a user might use the system a couple of times during a month for different reasons. Other systems will see the same user interacting multiple times per day. I've found that adding a time-based association to my scenarios helps me document usage in a more holistic way and helps the product team better understand the complexities that may otherwise be hard to uncover.

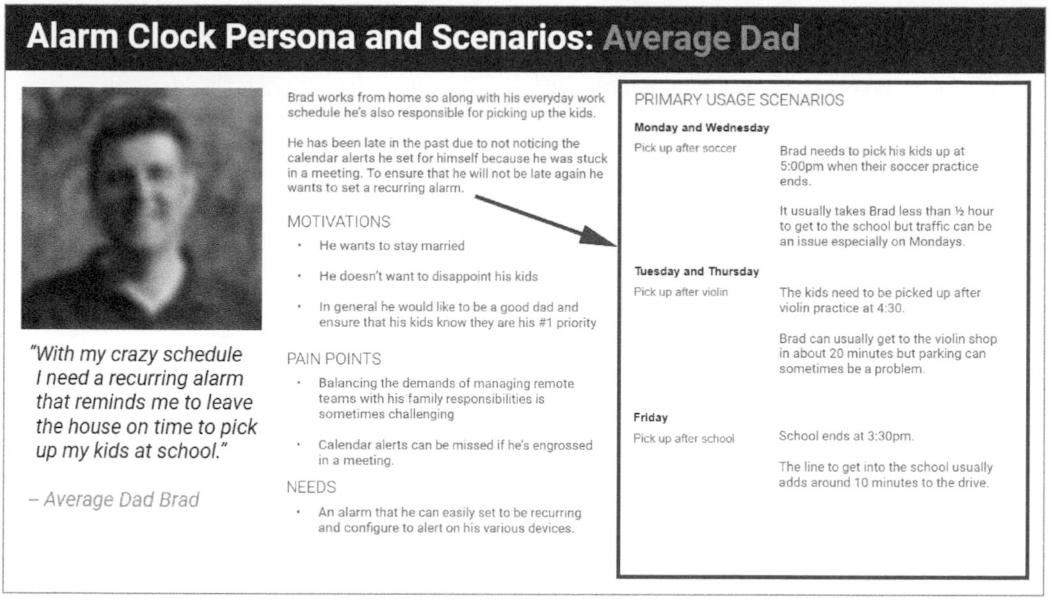

Alarm Clock Persona and Scenarios: Average Dad

Brad works from home so along with his everyday work schedule he's also responsible for picking up the kids.

He has been late in the past due to not noticing the calendar alerts he set for himself because he was stuck in a meeting. To ensure that he will not be late again he wants to set a recurring alarm.

MOTIVATIONS

- He wants to stay married
- He doesn't want to disappoint his kids
- In general he would like to be a good dad and ensure that his kids know they are his #1 priority

"With my crazy schedule I need a recurring alarm that reminds me to leave the house on time to pick up my kids at school."

– Average Dad Brad

PAIN POINTS

- Balancing the demands of managing remote teams with his family responsibilities is sometimes challenging
- Calendar alerts can be missed if he's engrossed in a meeting.

NEEDS

- An alarm that he can easily set to be recurring and configure to alert on his various devices.

PRIMARY USAGE SCENARIOS

Monday and Wednesday
Pick up after soccer — Brad needs to pick his kids up at 5:00pm when their soccer practice ends.

It usually takes Brad less than ½ hour to get to the school but traffic can be an issue especially on Mondays.

Tuesday and Thursday
Pick up after violin — The kids need to be picked up after violin practice at 4:30.

Brad can usually get to the violin shop in about 20 minutes but parking can sometimes be a problem.

Friday
Pick up after school — School ends at 3:30pm.

The line to get into the school usually adds around 10 minutes to the drive.

Figure 2.4: Documenting how your user's needs change in different contexts using scenarios can uncover new business opportunities.

However you document your scenarios, it is important to make sure they set the stage for the problem that needs to be solved.

Why do they need it?—prioritization and justification

Prioritization is something that often gets overlooked in the product design/development life cycle. In many cases, I've worked with teams that had no formal way of prioritizing the work and those decisions ended up being made by random people in the process. The classic example of this being a problem is when a salesperson comes back from a tradeshow with something hot and new that *must* be designed and built ASAP. The purpose of working together as a team to define your goals, strategies, OKRs, etc., is to provide a solid direction based on the best information the team has. The prioritization effort should work the same way, and if done well will clarify the plan for the product roadmap. This doesn't mean there won't be changes along the way. It means that those changes should be thought of as amendments to your team's constitution, should be considered carefully in terms of how this new idea will impact your OKRs, and should have buy-in from the rest of the team.

There are three main priority groupings you'll want to consider:

- **Personas based on their value to your organization.**
  Often this is purely a financial prioritization but, in some cases, your main goal might simply be the acquisition of new users, generating more page views, or some other indirect measurement.

- **Scenarios based on their value to the persona.**
  In this case, the goal is to gain clarity about what tasks are most important to your various personas. If you have trouble with this, try starting off with three main groupings: Essential, Nice to Have, and Can Live Without.

- **Use cases based on their value to the scenario.**
  Is mobile usage more important in this scenario than desktop? Is a noisy environment most likely to be the case for your highest-priority users? Will outdoor usage represent a large portion of user engagements? If so, these are use cases you'll want to move to the top of your list.

How will they use it?—use cases

Now that the team has an understanding of who the users are and what they need to be able to do, it's time to dig in and explore how the system is going to help the user complete the tasks listed in the scenarios. It's important to remember at this stage that we are talking about an iterative process. This first pass at creating use cases isn't meant to be the final solution. It is an exercise meant to help get your head in the game.

The role of the use case is to document in detail how the user will interact with the system and how the system will respond at each step of the process. Use cases also allow us to consider where the user will interact with the system. If the scenario states that the user needs to buy a birthday gift for their child, you may have many use cases. One example might be searching from their home computer. Another use case might be searching while commuting on the train using their mobile device. There can be many other variations as well.

Figure 2.5 shows how the basic use case format works and how this part of the process leads to a very detailed description of how a system could potentially work.

The key points to remember when creating a use case include:

- Work fast. Don't spend a lot of time trying to come up with the perfect solution. Once you get a draft of an approach down you can iterate on it to make it better. Keep in mind that not everything will be obvious at this stage, so if you sense that your progress is slowing down just move on. When you create wireframes, you'll find a lot of holes in your original use case and that is exactly how this process is supposed to work.

- Stick with a simple format. If you do this part right, each line of your use case will become one wireframe. All the wireframes that you create to illustrate a use case become a storyboard. Many times, I'll use the text from the written use case as annotation in my completed storyboards to help product owners, designers, and developers understand the solution.

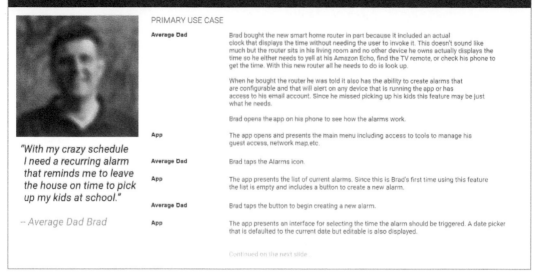

Alarm Clock Use Case: Average Dad - Pick up from Soccer

Figure 2.5: Detailed use cases are the foundation of good wireframes. Usually each step in a use case will become its own wireframe in the storyboard.

Here is a quick illustration of what the format looks like.

Step 1) The user takes an action
Step 2) The system responds by . . .
Step 3) The user takes another action
Step 4) The system responds by . . .

After you have a rough pass and feel like it's a good first attempt, use that to begin sketching your solution.

This is an important time to remember that although I'm describing all this in a step-wise process, it is better to think of each step as a tool in a toolbox that you will use when appropriate. I mention this now because there are many times when I find whiteboarding a solution or sketching one on paper to be a good first step instead of writing a use case. Sometimes I use the whiteboard drawings as a foundation to create a use case and vice versa. I usually do both, though, because writing engages a different part of my brain than whiteboarding does so I usually discover things I might have missed if I only did one or the other.

When Will We Design and Build It?: The Product Roadmap

A product roadmap serves as a timeline that helps all the various team members understand what the team is expected to deliver and when. A well-maintained roadmap can help the sales team confidently discuss upcoming features with prospective clients. The roadmap is also essential to helping investors and board members understand how the money spent is translating into value for the company. A roadmap that is ill-informed will cause friction between teams and team members, create the possibility that the sales team will be pitching vaporware, and mislead investors.

Creating a product roadmap sounds like it might be simple if we have already defined the highest-priority use cases, but roadmaps are much more complicated than just dropping your items on the calendar based on priority.

In order to create a meaningful roadmap, you'll need to have representatives of your design and development teams involved to break down the use cases into their various components. This needs to be done so that prerequisites, codependences, and risks can be identified and so that design and development estimates can be assigned to each component. It is entirely possible that during this process you'll find items that need more research, are impossible to estimate meaningfully, or otherwise don't end up fully defined. As frustrating as that can be, it is much better to know that at this phase of the game and adjust for it than to discover this type of issue after making promises to senior leadership or investors.

If you have a high-priority item that needs more research, add research to the plan and adjust your timelines. If you have an item that the team doesn't feel comfortable estimating, you may need to set up a meeting to break down that item further. This is all the grunt work of creating a great experience. It's not all colors and animation. Sometimes the best thing you can do for your users is to create realistic plans for your product and release valuable features that function as expected on a predictable schedule.

After you have a detailed view of the priority, time, and effort needed to create the various elements of each use case, the team can begin the process of organizing the work on the roadmap, as featured in Figure 2.6.

As I mentioned earlier, getting your team to buy in to the plan of action is very important. The roadmap is one tool to help facilitate discussions that will hopefully lead to team understanding and buy-in.

The product roadmap provides essential visibility into the plan for what will get designed and built and when each element falls into the product team's schedule. This helps everyone in the company align around what needs to be done and how to best support those efforts. Your roadmap should be broken down into time chunks that are meaningful

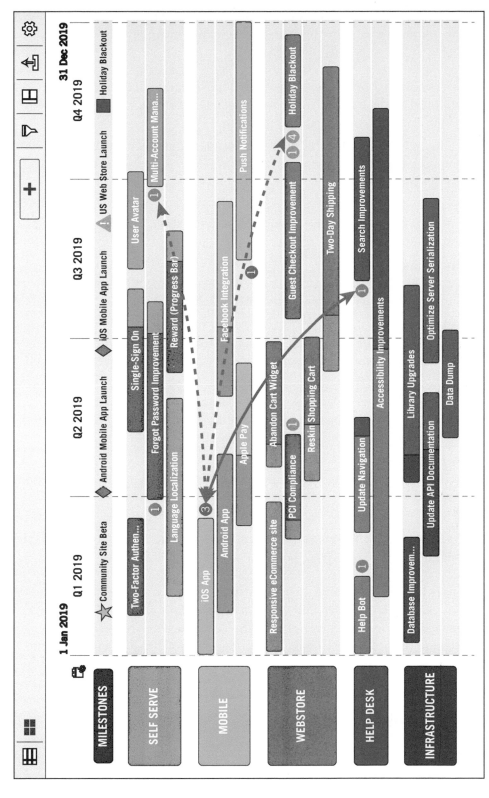

Figure 2.6: Roadmaps help communicate the product plan in a way that the entire team will be able to see and provide feedback on the high-level milestones.

to your team. That might mean that it's broken down into sprints, weeks, months, etc. Along with time frames, a roadmap might break down into the following swim lanes.

Research
All the activities meant to provide context for your team should fall into this swim lane. Everything from market and competitive research to user research.

UX
Taxonomy, IA, interaction design, wireframes, prototypes, and usability testing all fit into this category. Depending on your organization, you may group some of the other swim lanes into this one as well.

Graphic Design
Branding, visual hierarchy, colors, fonts, composition, consistency, texture, and style guides all fall into this swim lane.

Backend Development
Server-related code, configuration, management, and monitoring all fall into this swim lane. This also relates to model and controller-related code.

Frontend Development
HTML, CSS, and JavaScript are the primary aspects of front-end development for a website. View layer markup and code or anything in the presentation layer of an application will also fall into this swim lane.

QA
Activities that are related to testing the system to ensure that it functions as expected and that new code doesn't break pre-existing functionality belong here.

Readiness Coordination
New feature awareness, training, testing, and customer awareness initiatives are essential in this swim lane.

Analytics
All efforts to track, monitor, analyze, and communicate performance metrics should be tracked in this lane.

It's important to think of each lane as an activity rather than a role. Most companies do not have people in each of these roles. Startups usually have only a handful of people, and those employees are covering many roles. If you think of these as activities instead, you'll be in a good position to cover all the essential items even if you are just a team of one.

How will it work?—journey maps/wireframes/ prototypes/testing/iterations

Journey maps
Journey maps are another tool that can be useful when trying to quickly document how a user moves through a process or when you want to quickly iterate on new solutions before

committing to the time necessary to create wireframes. They can be used for everything from a single task flow to documenting an entire omnichannel user experience. Journey maps can be as simple as just illustrating the flow or as complex as including what users are thinking and what their emotional state is at each step in the process.

My rule for what method I use depends on what the map will be used for. If it's just a tool for iterating on potential flows, I will use the simplest version possible. Sometimes that ends up being a whiteboard in a workshop, and other times it's a Lucidchart document.

If, on the other hand, the map will be used to communicate user sentiment along with illustrating the flow to a customer or executive team, then I'll create the more complicated and illustrative version using Sketch or something similar.

Either way, it is important to remember that it is just a tool and once you start seeing diminishing returns on your efforts to create and iterate on the journey map, it's likely time to move on to creating wireframes.

It's important to note that I don't always create a journey map. Sometimes it is easier to write up a use case and then move straight to wireframes. Sometimes I start with a wireframe sketch, then draw out a hybrid journey map/storyboard. Instead of making this simple for you, I'm being honest and saying that you need to be open to changing things up so that you don't become too dogmatic and get stuck doing things just for the sake of doing them. If you believe you will derive value from it, by all means, include it for that project. If you think you can make better progress using another method, do that. If it turns out you were wrong and you end up needing a journey map, go back and create it. I see many teams create them because they are a cool-looking deliverable, but if they are not backed by solid data all their power to communicate might actually be misleading your team. If you don't have the data, don't use this artifact. If you have the data, carefully craft your journey map to ensure it tells the story of that data like the example in Figure 2.7.

Wireframes

If you have been following along you already know that all the things I cover in this book are simply tools you can use to understand and improve your user experience. UX is less of a process and more of a toolbox. UX isn't a silver bullet that is guaranteed to solve all problems. It's not a one-time investment. UX activities can lead to better business outcomes, but only if they are integrated into your business and thought of as part of a larger culture of iterative, research-driven design and development.

Wireframes are simply one tool in the box as well, but in many ways, I feel like they are 95% of what most people think of as UX design. I think that's because they are the easiest artifact to begin creating due to a large number of easy-to-use tools like Balsamiq,

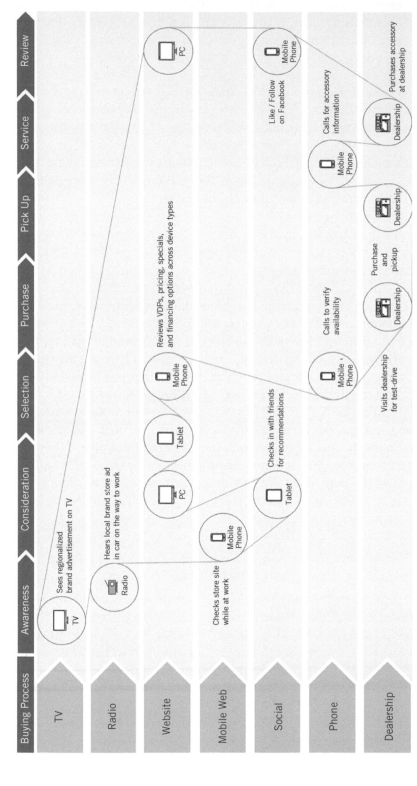

Figure 2.7: Journey maps can be a helpful way to illustrate how a user moves through the various stages of a process. It can also be misleading if it is not created off of solid data.

Axure, and Sketch. I also think it is because it's the most comfortable transition from other design fields.

Wireframes are an essential tool because they allow designers to communicate their intentions for how an information architecture will translate into a visual interface. They allow designers to experiment with various kinds of interactions so they can recommend the one that is the best for the job. Wireframes allow for the foundation for the visual hierarchy to be considered as well as text-based content. What wireframes don't do is explore color options, branding, photography, etc. Wireframes should be grayscale, with no photographs. They should be detailed enough to explore how the information architecture, taxonomy, basic visual hierarchy, interaction patterns, and text-based content all work together to support the users in completing their task.

The problem comes in when designers don't understand that adding color, photos, etc., distract from the foundational design concepts I mentioned previously. Remember—useful, usable, beautiful—in that order. You might have a terrible interaction or navigation system that gets completely ignored in a review meeting because the conversation gets derailed by how much everyone loves how the new logo and branding colors look.

Conversely, you might have a wonderful advancement in a key interaction that would save users time and reduce errors get trashed in a meeting because the CEO's mother doesn't like orange and it's included in this design option. I would love to tell you that the last one is an extreme example, but it actually happened to a team I worked with.

In the beginning wireframes should start off super simple and be focused on content, interactions, and information architecture. Many people overdesign their wireframes, defeating part of their purpose. As a design system matures, wireframes can include more detail.

Figure 2.8 illustrates some sample wireframes.

On the opposite end of the spectrum, when I work with students or interns to help them create their first set of wireframes, I've noticed that many oversimplify their screens. I've already covered the dangers of adding colors or otherwise spending too much time with other design elements, but oversimplification has its own set of dangers.

The most common and dangerous form of oversimplifying the wireframe is using placeholder text. "Content First Design" isn't a new concept, but it is one that is overlooked by many designers. In general, my recommendation is to include as much real and final content in your wireframes as is possible and take note of what you don't have so you can get it ASAP. The reason for this is that users need to be able to scan, read, and comprehend the content of your page to be able to make decisions about what to do and where to go next. If you have a bunch of placeholder content in the storyboards you are

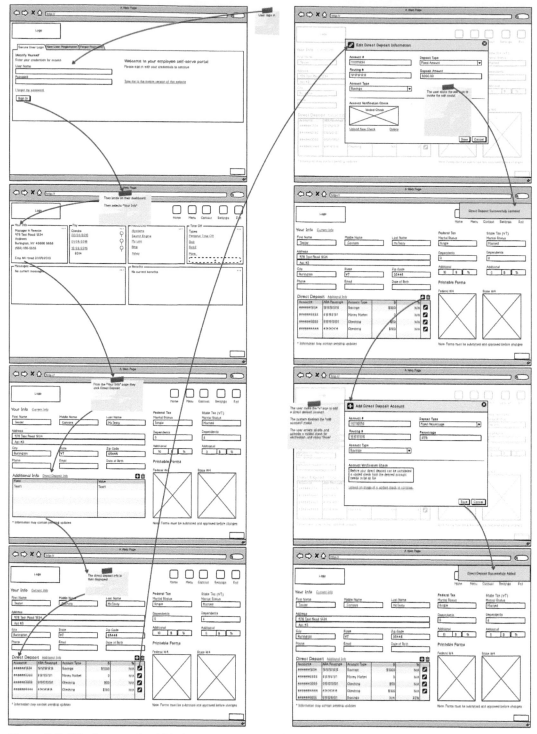

Figure 2.8: Wireframes should help your team and clients understand what your intentions are for improving the experience.

testing, you may not get an accurate picture of what real usage will look like. You will also be missing out on the value of having your participants provide feedback on what you believe to be compelling content. Testing isn't always cheap, so it is important to derive as much value as possible as early as possible.

Prototypes

A prototype is a demo of a specific piece of functionality that can be used for testing purposes. One of the simplest forms of a prototype is used in what is called a *first click test*. To set up this type of test you could use just one wireframe. In other cases, you might have several versions of that single wireframe so that you can test against each other to identify the one that is working best for your users.

The only code involved in this type of prototype is what is necessary to present the image to the user and the code needed to record where the user clicked. So that I don't need to manage any of that code, I use Optimal Workshop when I conduct a first click test. It also provides wonderful analytics so that it's easy to see what happened during your testing session. You can skip the high-tech approach altogether and do this test in person as well. Depending on the situation, I sometimes just bring my iPad with the JPEG open so the users can see the screen and point to where they would click. What I love about doing these tests in person is that I see their expressions as they review the design. I can see where they moved their finger to point first, then the subtle correction to where they end up pointing. I can also ask them follow-up questions to gather more context for the team.

Paper prototypes can be used for this purpose as well. Just print out the screen you want to test and give it to users with an explanation of the task they need to complete. They can simply use a pencil or marker to note where they would "click" first.

Paper prototypes are very fast to create and iterate on and they have a very low cost, so this makes them an ideal tool for early testing. When I'm working within a company as part of their full-time team, I'll often start this process with hand-drawn sketches, testing with other internal staff initially, and move my way up to computer-based wireframes once I feel pretty good that I'm on the right track.

Once I have a task flow completely illustrated in a storyboard, I'll often use that to test with users that match my target user demographics. At this point in the process, I'll usually use a clickable prototype. The simplest form of clickable prototype is made up of a bunch of screenshots, each on its own HTML page. The images are all "image mapped" with clickable hotspots that lead to the other screens in the storyboard. I've been using this method since the 1990s and it still works just fine today, but most designers will use a tool like InVision (www.invisionapp.com) to simplify this process. InVision is tightly integrated with industry-leading design tools like Sketch and has helpful collaboration tools as well. Whatever method you choose to do it technically, clickable prototypes are a great and inexpensive method of testing your solutions with real users.

In some cases, I'll go as far as coding the actual interactions in HTML, but I try to keep this to a minimum because testing at that level starts to erode the value of testing before committing to code in the first place. When I've done this in the past it was because the interactions were more complex/nonstandard, and I really wanted to make sure to get some data before making the final recommendation.

All these methods can be used with everything from very low-fidelity wireframes up to production-ready designs that include all the typography, colors, branding, and content. The only distinction is that you should wait to test with completed designs until after you have tested with low-fidelity designs so that you can validate the information architecture (IA), content, interaction design (IxD), and foundation of your visual hierarchy. Once those are in great shape, you are safe to spend the time and money on final design iterations.

Research

There are several different ways that you can go about conducting research to better understand your users. I've included descriptions of some of the most widely used methods in the following sections. It is outside the scope of this book to explain in detail how to conduct each of these types of research. My goal is to make sure you are aware of the key tools that you'll need to use so that you can choose the appropriate ones and learn more about each when the need arises.

Contextual inquiry

This is one of the most important and widely used testing methods. It is used to learn how users currently think about and execute common tasks. It is best to conduct this kind of testing in person at the location where the user interacts with the system you are going to be testing. This allows the tester to observe things that may otherwise go undocumented such as the users' disposition, their posture, their environmental conditions, and their unique methods of interacting with the system to complete their tasks.

Longitudinal studies

This method is used to learn how key measures of usability change over time and potentially how changes to the experience impact usage for the same user over a period of time. Because of the time and budget necessary for this type of study, I have most often conducted these using a combination by having the participants complete an initial assessment to establish a baseline, then have them answer a series of questions in a journal as they use the system over a period of time. This process can be conducted in a series of in-person interviews as well.

Ethnographic studies

This method is a comprehensive deep dive into the all-day, everyday living patterns of a specific user type including their interactions with the target system. These are conducted in person and are much less frequently used because of the time and budget required. The main advantage of ethnographic studies is that your team will gain a strong understanding of the participant's context for their usage of the target system. Your team will be exposed to the elements in the participant's life that lead to usage as well as those that interrupt, stop, or prevent usage. Combining this type of information with what you'll learn about their actual usage will provide a comprehensive view of the entire user journey. This type of research is especially helpful in documenting how cultural differences impact a system's usage.

Usability testing methods

Usability testing is one of the most important tools in the toolbox because the findings give your team vision into what is working and what is not. With this information, your team can identify the most important issues to address and plan all future efforts.

Once the testing sessions are complete, you'll need to carefully review all the data and distill it into an observations and recommendations document like the one in Figure 2.9. Usually, this will include issue prioritization as well as high-level effort estimates so that the team can easily begin to consider the next steps once they review your findings.

It's also important to provide the raw data so that others can verify your findings and conclusions.

Some of the most important testing methods I use are discussed in the following sections. This isn't a comprehensive list. Instead, I've provided the ones that I find most useful so that you can focus there first and dive into the rest once you are comfortable with these.

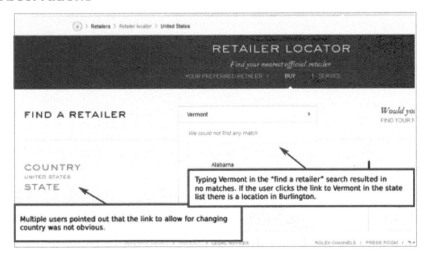

Figure 2.9: Observations and recommendations documents help communicate the findings of your research in a way that executive team members and developers will be able to take action on.

Card sorting

Card sorting tests are used to understand how your taxonomy (naming and grouping) and information architecture choices are performing with real users.

You will use an open card sort if you want your participants to organize your content into groups that they believe make sense. The participants would then name the content groups they have created. By using this approach you'll get the deepest insight into how your users think your information should be organized.

A closed card sort uses the same process as the open card sort, but your team will provide predetermined and named categories that the users will need to use when sorting your content. You would want to use this if you have already determined the best high-level categories but want to learn more about how your users will organize your content within those groupings.

So far, I haven't found a better tool than what Optimal Workshop (www.optimalworkshop.com/optimalsort) offers for card sorting. The analysis tools help to provide vision into the results and the time savings easily pay for the cost of running the test with their service.

First click testing

As I mentioned previously, a first click test consists of an image of your screen that you want to test, a system that will record the user clicks such as Optimal Workshop's chalk mark test (www.optimalworkshop.com/chalkmark) or a moderator that will record the user attempts as they happen. Either way, what is important here is that the team gains a solid understanding of where the participants think they should click first to complete their task. If your users know where to click, that is a good indication that the page design and interactions are doing their job well. If users don't know where to click first, you'll want to make sure your page only includes the items that are essential to the key user behaviors. Then you'll want to ensure that your taxonomy and information architecture are supporting the users on their journey.

Finally, it's possible that the content and interactions are not helping to inform/direct the users as they try to complete their task, so make sure to consider that as you work to resolve any issues.

Time on task

This type of test is used to quantify the total amount of time it takes users to complete a given task. This is a great way to help benchmark your system. You can also test how long it takes users to complete the same task on competitor systems. With that information, you'll be able to measure and monitor your status on this metric over time. If it turns out that the performance you measure is great when compared to the competition, share that with your sales and marketing teams. If not, then you can prioritize improvements with your team.

To conduct this type of test all you need to do is time each user as they complete the same test. If there are any wildly different results, review those carefully to ensure that the testing method or some other external variable didn't make that result invalid.

It is also important to track the number of errors the user makes during the process. If users complete their task very fast but with many errors, that isn't a great result. Conversely, if your new approach helps users reduce the time it takes to complete a task and reduces the error rate, you know you have a solution that you need to promote. I find recording these tests to be very helpful so that you can verify your results at a later date and review the usage more critically to ensure that you understand the results.

Clicks to complete assessment

Clicks to complete testing is similar to time on task but in this case, you'll be measuring the number of clicks (or taps, swipes, etc.) it takes to complete a specific task. If you can reduce the number of interactions a user needs to complete without increasing the error rate, you have likely created an improved experience. This is another great benchmark to share with your team.

Test facilitation methods

Often, the method you choose to facilitate your sessions will be determined by the budget and the availability of local participants. Many times, it is just not practical to bring users that match your target demographic into your office for the session. If I have the choice, I'll always choose in-person sessions. Direct observation allows me to catch reactions I might otherwise miss and make more subtle adjustments to my testing method.

Unmoderated sessions

Unmoderated in this context means a researcher isn't there in person or online to conduct the test with the participant. Instead, users are invited to participate in the testing session usually via email and given a link to the survey so they can begin. The session is documented with video and audio recordings of users completing tasks and self-reporting on success as well as their other perceptions. Often the system will record findings to various question types, making analysis and documentation like what you see in Figure 2.10 much easier.

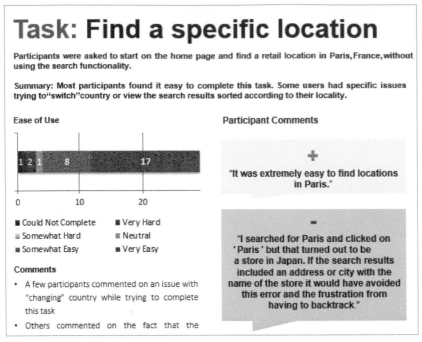

Figure 2.10: Once you have analyzed the results you can create a report like the one illustrated in this figure to help communicate the findings with the rest of your team

Moderated sessions

This type of testing takes place in person where the moderator asks questions or presents tasks to the participant. The participant is recorded answering the questions and/or attempting to complete the tasks like what is illustrated in Figure 2.11.

Remote moderated sessions

A remote session is conducted with the moderator in a different location than the participant, connected via a video conferencing solution. My favorite tool for this is Zoom.us because it is simple for all types of users to connect with and use and provides high-quality recordings even when connected to a relatively slow internet connection. The moderator asks questions or presents tasks to the participant and the participant is recorded answering the questions and/or attempting to complete the tasks.

If you are testing a desktop system, Zoom can record both the screen and the users at the same time so you can capture both the usage and the user reactions as they complete their task like what is illustrated in Figure 2.12. If you are testing a mobile solution, you'll need to use another tool to mirror your mobile device onto your desktop so that it can be recorded.

Figure 2.11: Moderated sessions can take place onsite where the user will interact with the system being tested, at a pre-arranged meeting place, or at a specialized testing facility like this one.

Figure 2.12: Remote moderated testing services provided by companies like `Applause.com` are some of the most cost-effective methods I know of for getting actionable feedback from customers that match your target demographic.

- For iOS devices, you can use Airbeam.tv: `www.airbeam.tv/mirror-iphone-ipadscreen/mac-windows`

- For Android devices, you can use the vysor.io Chrome plugin: `vysor.io`

Once you have your mirroring set up, you can use the controls within Zoom to record the screen and the user at the same time if the user has a webcam.

Recruiting

Whatever testing method you are planning, one of the hardest and most costly parts of the process is usually recruiting. There are various companies that can help you recruit participants and the time and cost associated is directly related to the type of user you need to test with and how specialized that need is.

If you are testing a shopping solution like Amazon you might be able to get away with relatively inexpensive recruiting because the demographics for that type of usage are very broad and you will likely learn a lot from the average user.

If, on the other hand, you are testing a clinical information resource for doctors you'll need to test with actual doctors, and they are harder to identify and incentivize. In many cases when working with companies that have a very specialized need, they will identify customers that they can work with. That can be a good approach and I've managed customer advisory boards as well, but it is important to make sure you rotate the membership in your advisory board regularly so that you are not always talking to the same exact users and so that you can ensure that the advisory board is made up of users that represent the ever-changing needs of the business versus staying with the same users that were identified at the beginning of the process.

Your sales and marketing team is a good place to start if you want to create a customer advisory board. You'll likely be able to gather 10 solid participants, and that's what you'll likely need for a lot of your everyday testing needs. Rotating those members every six months to a year will help keep the feedback you gather fresh, honest, and on target for what you are trying to learn.

If I need to recruit outside my advisory board, I'll use one of only a few approaches depending on the size of the client I'm working with and how specific their need is.

The first approach is the LinkedIn/Network approach. This honestly doesn't work often, but since it is free it is worth trying. If you are socially active in your industry you will have a better chance of making this work. If going to meetups and networking in general isn't your thing, this approach isn't for you.

The next best thing is using a service such as UserInterviews (www.userinterviews.com/researcher) to handle the recruiting for you. My experience has been that these mid-level recruiting services work well for basic testing and can most often provide me with great candidates, usually when I'm working on a consumer-facing system. I've also been able to use them for more advanced business-to-business testing but for those, I recommend paying more and relying on a premium service such as Applause App Quality, Inc. (www.applause.com). You get what you pay for, and most of my biggest clients have used Applause as their testing service of choice. My experience has been that you cannot go wrong using Applause because it has the biggest network and the most professional services available. I've worked with them to service some of the world's biggest and most high-profile companies including Google, Rolex, Samsung, Michael Kors, Hyundai, and many others, and they have always delivered even when testing with participants across 10 countries simultaneously.

Once you settle on how you are going to recruit, you'll need to prepare a screener. A screener is simply a list of questions used to qualify potential participants based on the demographics and usage patterns that are required for your test.

When writing your screener, it is important that you first identify anything that will disqualify a participant. Make sure to present those questions first in your screener. From there your questions should be organized to help prioritize the remaining participants. Ideally, you'll be working with users who meet all your criteria but sometimes it isn't possible and, in those cases, you'll want to be working with the best you can get. By following this process, you'll end up with at least the following groups to work with.

Unqualified participants

Those that fundamentally do not qualify. An example of this would be if you were testing a new cloud management tool and needed participants that have cloud configuration experience. If candidates answer no to the question relating to that experience, they wouldn't be qualified to participate.

Minimally qualified participants

Continuing with the preceding example, someone who has just started managing cloud configurations might qualify but they won't have a lot of real-world experience, so their feedback might be limited. On the other hand, if you are trying to understand the thoughts of inexperienced users, this group might be a good fit.

Well-qualified participants

These participants have substantial experience in cloud management and configuration, so their feedback is likely to be very relevant to your team.

You may end up with more groupings, but it's helpful if you have at least these three to work from. You'll get the best results if the members of your test group are all well qualified.

When writing your questions make sure they are not leading. You don't want potential participants to know what you are looking for in your screener. You just want honest answers, so do your best to provide enough variation in your questions so that users won't know exactly what the "right" answers might be.

You can download an example screener from www.chaostoconcept.com/screener.

Iterating

I've included iterating here at the end but in reality, you can and should be iterating on all parts of your UX pipeline as your business goals shift and as you gather more accurate information. Your strategies, objectives, personas, scenarios, use cases, wireframes, etc., all should be in a continuous cycle of iterative improvement.

This is where my earlier commentary on creating lightweight artifacts comes into focus. If you have a designer, contractor, or agency create artifacts that are overly designed or in a format that your internal team cannot maintain, you will be stuck in the bad position of either not updating them or having to re-create them so they will work for your team. Do your best to consider this early in the process so you can adjust before it becomes a real problem for your team.

MAKE IT BEAUTIFUL

"Design is the silent ambassador to your brand."

—Paul Rand

This chapter won't teach you to be a graphic designer. It will teach you how to evaluate a design from a user experience point of view and provide you with further reading if you want to learn more about how to be a graphic designer.

With all that research and planning from the previous chapters out of the way, you might think the design work is mostly complete. In reality, what we have from all the previous work is a solid foundation on which we'll build out the rest of the design. If we were building a physical structure that visitors would experience in person, at this phase we would have a concrete foundation and all the ceilings, walls, and floors framed out like what is illustrated in Figure 3.1. That being said, we wouldn't have any paint, flooring, windows, doors, fixtures, or furnishings chosen or in place yet. This is a loose analogy because digital designers may have more control over the final user experience than interior designers do, but the idea that a research-based and user-centered foundation should be in place for the digital designer to work from is a solid comparison.

Choose your own adventure . . . continue reading from here to learn about why design is more important than many people believe, or skip ahead to the tactical design information on page 62.

Design is often thought of as being very abstract and more of an art than a science, but that is not at all the case. One of the things about working in this industry that is the most frustrating is that many designers approach their work and promote their process as if it is magical as well.

Figure 3.1: This image shows the steps of remodeling a basement room.

I won't deny that there aren't magical moments in design just like there are in programming, engineering, and every other profession, but most of those magical moments come out of a solid repeatable process that structures the problem in a way that allows the team to invent novel and exceptional solutions that impact the user in positive ways never before imagined. To those observing from outside the process, there is no doubt that the result appears magical just like the result of an organ transplant surgery appears magical, but in reality, it is the result of countless hours of teamwork, preparation, process, and skillful execution.

When I worked at UpToDate Inc. (the world's #1 clinical information resource for doctors), the teams would remind each other regularly that the mistakes we made could impact actual medical outcomes. There is no better motivator when it comes to emphasizing how important it is to do your job well than realizing that the quality of your work may directly impact another person's health. The team focus on creating information and experiences that would help doctors accurately diagnose and care for their patients is why 1.7 million physicians worldwide and those orbiting the earth in the International Space Station use UpToDate.

While it's true that some of our work may actually save lives, most of our work will fall into a category I call "saving life." When I say UX work done well "saves life," what I mean is that our work reduces errors and the amount of time it takes users to complete their tasks. In this way, we are saving them time and potentially giving them opportunities they would have otherwise missed. Since life is measured in time, we are literally saving life by making systems more efficient.

You might be thinking this is a cute little play on words, but I assure you the real-world impact can be tremendous. Consider high school students and their parents completing an online financial aid form. This is a high-stress task and one that requires information to be entered correctly and in a timely manner. Financial information is special in that many people are intimidated when interacting with any sort of official institution when money is the primary topic. This enhanced level of stress causes people to have a harder time comprehending instructions, making it more likely that they might make mistakes. As a person who worked as a financial aid counselor at a university for three years, I can tell you from personal experience that the compounding lifetime impact of making a mistake during this process can be truly catastrophic. Enhancements to a system like this that improve the number of people who complete their applications on time and without errors may not literally save lives, but it certainly "saves life."

A less dramatic example is when a UX research project clearly identifies that functionality the team previously believed to be essential turns out to be trivial from the user's point of view. I love this type of finding because I can clearly see the impacts within my workplace. The product team no longer needs to spend time specifying the work. The designers don't need to make accommodations for the new functionality in the UI, and the developers don't need to waste their time building something no one wants and won't use. Without the worry of having to add that new feature, the team is free to capitalize on other opportunities and maybe even get to leave work on time to see their loved ones.

So how can we use design at this phase of the project to save some life? There is no easy way to organize all the elements of a quality design into a linear process. The design process is made up of many micro-iterations that include all the various elements of the design pushing and pulling, shifting, and squeezing together into one cohesive presentation of the information and interactions required to meet the business and user objectives.

Instead of trying to walk you through a step-by-step guide on how to design a user interface (UI), I'm going to discuss the various elements that come into play when designing screens to help users scan, read, comprehend, and interact with the content. Understanding the key issues that negatively impact users as well as the best ways to deal with those issues will allow you to create better experiences regardless of what industry you are in. Whatever brand guidelines or design style you work from, you'll also need to make sure you have accounted for all those considerations to help ensure your design works well for the end user.

Scannability, Readability, Comprehension

A layout that is scannable is one where the user's eye can quickly and accurately travel through the layout, scanning for the best content or interaction to help them move to the next step in their task.

The examples in Figure 3.2 and Figure 3.3 illustrate how the same content can be more or less scannable.

Classes:
Hack a Broken Robot
3:30 pm to 5:00 pm Friday
Drop-in class. Use parts from one robot to create a different robot.

Homeschool Space Bots
1:30 pm to 3:00 pm Friday
Program your robot to get to the broken space ship and bring it back to base.

Arduino Cars
12:00 pm to 3:00 pm Saturday
Using a custom 3d printed chassis and an Arduino you'll build your own self-driving toy car.

Sumo bots
3:00 pm to 6:00 pm Saturday
Drop-in class. Create a robot that will push another robot out of the Sumo ring!

Figure 3.2: In this example you can certainly still read the content, but the lack of design makes it hard to scan the information.

Classes

Friday

Hack a Broken Robot - Drop-in class
3:30 pm to 5:00 pm
Use parts from one robot to create a different robot.

Homeschool Space Bots
1:30 pm to 3:00 pm
Program your robot to get to the broken space ship and bring it back to base.

Saturday

Arduino Cars
12:00 pm to 3:00 pm
Using a custom 3d printed chassis and an Arduino you'll build a self-driving toy car.

Sumo bots - Drop-in class
3:00 pm to 6:00 pm
Create a robot that will push another robot out of the Sumo ring!

Figure 3.3: The same content as Figure 3.2 but with some basic design applied to it to create a stronger, more scannable, visual hierarchy

Using the Inverted Pyramid Model for Content

Over the years there have been many studies that talk about how users don't want to read a lot of content online. That is only true when users are still in the search phase of their interaction. Once they have found what they want, they are happy to read and view content.

The inverted pyramid writing style comes from journalism. The idea is that the wide top of the inverted pyramid should contain the main details—who, what, where, why, when, and how—along with the "hook" that will draw users in to read more as is illustrated in Figure 3.4.

Figure 3.4: The inverted pyramid content model represents a classic content model that is rooted in early newspapers.

This approach can apply to structuring your website and its content. In this case you need your navigation to follow the inverted pyramid model and your content to follow a standard pyramid as shown in Figure 3.5. What this means in practical terms is that at the beginning of your user journey, navigation and content that supports the user in their navigation decisions get the most importance while detailed content is minimized and that relationship inverts as users progress through their journey. The theory is that while users are still trying to find what they are looking for is not the best time to present the user with all the content you have on every possible subject. Once users have finally navigated to the content they are looking for, that is the time for them to get everything you have to offer on the subject.

Dual Pyramid Model of Navigation and Content

Broad navigation   at the top

Just enough content at the top

Just enough navigation at the bottom

Broad content   at the bottom

Figure 3.5: The dual pyramid navigation/content model leverages the traditional inverted content model while layering navigation patterns on top to help users when needed throughout their journey.

That approach works in a pretty straightforward way for ecommerce, news, or other content-heavy systems, but what about B2B, SAAS, Enterprise, and other non–content-heavy sites or applications?

In those cases both pyramids still exist, but they are squashed to the point where there is a lot more overlap and it is harder to see the distinctions.

If we think of using gmail.com in this way, what we'll see upon signing in is that the designers have provided us with just enough information to be able to take the next step in the process as seen in Figure 3.6.

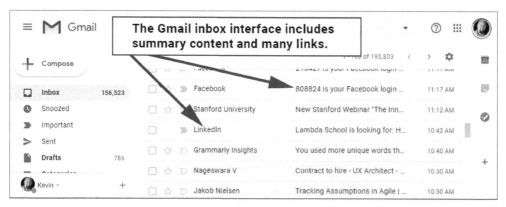

Figure 3.6: The Gmail List View illustrates the small point of the top of the content pyramid and the wide bottom of the navigation pyramid coexisting at the beginning of the journey.

The most prominent item in the visual hierarchy is the list of emails. They don't show us all the content of each email because at this point in the user journey all that would do is slow us down. What is there is short but important in helping us scan, read, comprehend, and make navigation decisions so that we can continue with our journey quickly and efficiently. At this point we are at the widest part of the navigation pyramid and at the narrowest point of the content pyramid.

Once we make a selection and click to view an email, the interface changes so that the full content of the email can be seen. The content is the highest priority in the visual hierarchy of the page and the navigation has been reduced to what you see in the left column. The entirety of what we saw right after we signed in has been reduced to a single icon, some text (inbox), and a number (the number of unopened emails in your inbox) as shown in Figure 3.7. While reading the details of an email, we are at the widest part of the content pyramid while simultaneously at the narrowest part of the navigation pyramid.

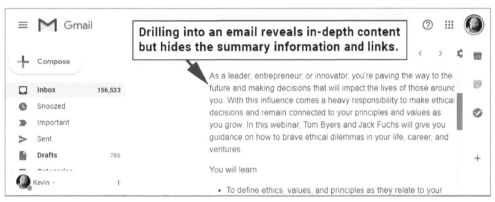

Figure 3.7: The Gmail Email Detail View illustrates the wide bottom of the content pyramid and the small point of the navigation pyramid coexisting at the end of the journey.

For a service like Gmail the entire transition in focus between navigation and content only takes one click. For an ecommerce site it may take four or more clicks, but the concept is the same.

Alignment and the Grid

The grid is the industry standard method of aligning items in your composition. Essentially the grid is a system of guides used to help designers place items within a design layout as seen in Figure 3.8. It has its origins in print-based design with the added bonus for screen-based design being that it aids in the responsive design and development process.

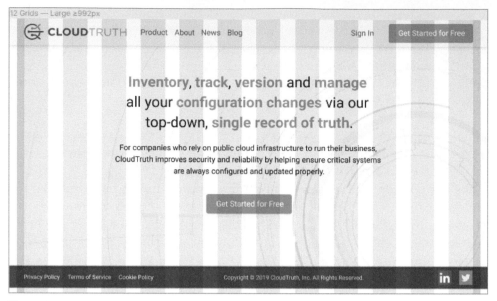

Figure 3.8: The grid is left "on" in this Figma design (a design tool like Adobe Illustrator or Sketch) of a landing page. The grid plays a prominent role in design because it provides a clear way to establish the structure of a design.

Google's Material Design website has a great breakdown of its grid system and how it gets used across a wide variety of device types. The grid as a foundation for your design isn't one of the areas where I recommend getting too creative. Using the grid system that is standard for Google's Material Design or something similar will be a great starting point and will help ensure that your design will work well across many device types.

You can learn more about Material design at:

material.io/design/layout/responsive-layout-grid.html#

The grid breaks your layout into margins, columns, and gutters. The margins are the empty spaces on the left and right of your layout meant to create visual separation between the edge of the device screen and the content to help guide the eye as the user scans the page. The columns are the main content areas within the layout. They are separated from one another by gutters that help delineate the major content areas from one another and help users successfully scan the page as they search for their desired content or interactions.

The maximum number of columns that can be displayed varies based on device resolution, with smaller resolutions having 4 columns and the largest resolutions having 12. It is important to understand that your content can span multiple columns. It's possible to have a 12-column grid that displays the page content in 2 columns. The first column might span 4 columns on a large resolution to contain the nav, while the other column spans 8 columns and contains the main content area. The user would only see 2 columns in this case because each of the columns would be made up by spanning the number of columns required to create a full screen layout with only 2 columns.

All of this is important because alignment is one of the key elements of a design that will promote scannability within a layout as shown in Figure 3.9.

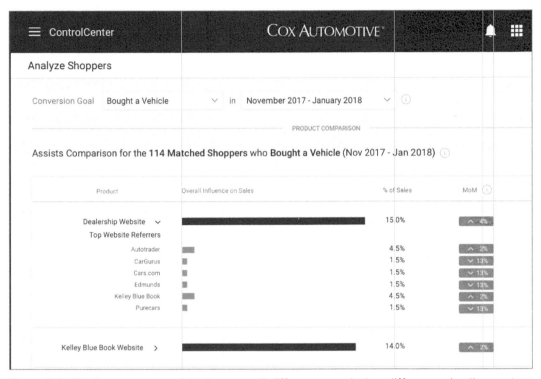

Figure 3.9: The human eye can detect very small differences, and when differences in alignment are observed our brains process that difference to see if it represents another level in the visual hierarchy.

For some users slight alignment issues will go unnoticed. For other users, misaligned items due to poor design consistency will have a negative impact on their perception of the brand. In extreme cases, mistakes in alignment can result in comprehension errors. This most often happens when decimal points in numbers are not aligned.

Visual Hierarchy

At its core, visual hierarchy is about prioritizing and organizing information and interactions within your composition.

I believe it's best to keep the design grayscale (a range of gray shades from white to black) during this part of the process to ensure that your hierarchy is designed well. If you can create a strong visual hierarchy without the use of color, your design will be more usable for anyone with a visual disability and you'll have an easier time spotting issues while you work out the details of your design. Many professionals will disagree with me on this, so don't be surprised if you get pushback, but it is the best way I know to create a strong hierarchy that works for the broadest range of users.

One very quick example of why this approach is helpful can be seen when designing status alerts into data tables as shown in Figure 3.10. If you simply use color to indicate the status, users who have issues perceiving color will be unable to see that status is indicated at all. Other users may misunderstand the status and be misled by your design.

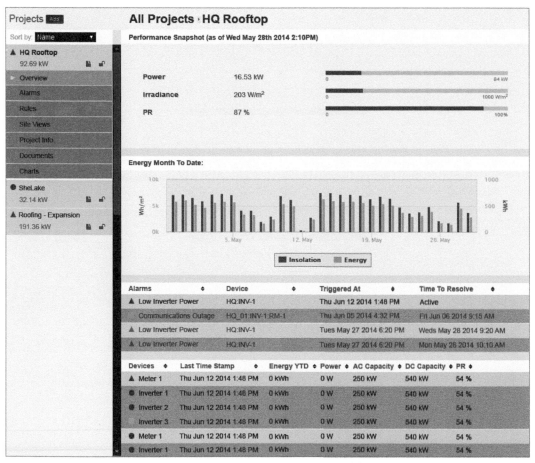

Figure 3.10: In this example, the data table includes status indicators that use color and shape to help users comprehend their meaning.

If you designed this table using grayscale shades first, you would obviously see that using color alone to indicate status is insufficient. My solution for this type of situation is to always use both shape and color to indicate status so that a wider range of users will be able to comprehend the meaning. It's also important to include a key so that users don't have to guess what the color and shape combinations mean. Colors and even shapes have different meanings in different cultures, so a key will help to eliminate those concerns.

If you started off designing this table in color, it is very likely that you wouldn't even know there was a problem in the first place unless a user pointed it out during testing or via a feedback method. In reality, though, mistakes like this end up existing within systems for years impacting users and never getting resolved.

Composition

Each of the elements that we are discussing in this chapter roughly aligns with its own college-level class. Those classes take place over a 15-week period so there really is no way for me to cover all of that material in this book. What I can do, though, is highlight some of the key elements of composition as they relate to ensuring that your design is usable, and point you to some more in-depth resources as we move along.

For screen-based design the first element of composition that needs to be covered is "the fold." The fold is a term that relates back to the days when print newspapers were the main way of sharing information. Those papers were folded and the most important information for the day was featured above that fold to help ensure it was seen. In screen-based design, being above the fold can be thought of as the content that will fit in the first screenful of information before having to scroll.

If you want to waste a bunch of time you can go read many articles on the internet stating that the fold is no longer relevant, that it's dead, or that it no longer exists in this world of many device form factors, etc.

There is a lot of information that will sound compelling but ignores one key element of the human experience: we can't read, comprehend, or interact with something we cannot see. If you combine that with research from the Nielsen Norman Group (two of the most respected early pioneers of UX a group you should research if you haven't ready) that states that 57% of viewing time is above the fold, with 74% being within the first two screenfuls of content, you'll see that it is essential that you understand where the fold(s) are in your designs and that you use that information to promote the most valuable content. Users do scroll more now than they did 15 years ago, but the impact of the fold continues today and is clearly shown in in Figure 3.11. It is hard to design for, but important nonetheless.

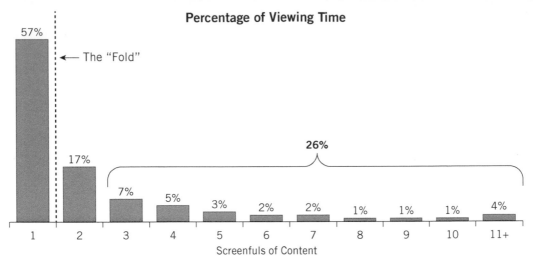

Figure 3.11: The fold is important because users are less likely to act on what they cannot see.

The reason people don't want to believe that the concept of the fold is important despite what research shows is that designing for it has become very difficult. Designing with the fold as a consideration is hard because of the ever-growing range of screen sizes and resolutions that sites/apps are required to work on. Notice I didn't say "ever-growing range of devices." That was purposeful because the difference between devices and resolutions is something else that is important to understand if you are ever going to hope to account for the fold in your design work.

It's not uncommon for designers to work on large, state-of-the-art, high-resolution monitors. If that's what you use all day it is fair to say that you might think that's what everyone else uses as well. That's simply not true. So how do you know what size screens your users have? Google Analytics and other tools like it can provide you with this type of information. If you don't have an analytics system in place, add it to your short list of things to get done because it is essential to be able to review quantitative information about how users interact with your system. Without it you are driving with one eye closed. If you are not regularly talking with users who match your key demographics as well, you are driving with both eyes closed.

If you look at a standard report on the top resolutions used with your system, you'll see something that looks like Figure 3.12.

If you look at that report, it will be tempting to say "OK, great . . . most of my users are working with monitors that are at least X×X in size" and then start designing for that. Here's where the differences between device, resolution, and user preferences all collide. There is a secondary measurement that you need to account for to really get a clear

Screen Resolution	Users	New Users	Sessions	Bounce Rate	Pages / Session	Avg. Session Duration	Transactions	Revenue	Ecommerce Conversion Rate
	15,984 %of Total 100.00% (15,984)	13,511 %of Total 100.07% (13,502)	19,396 %of Total 100.00% (19,396)	43.00% Avg for View 43.00% (0.00%)	4.67 Avg for View 4.67 (0.00%)	00:02:57 Avg for View 00:02:57 (0.00%)	45 %of Total 100.00% (45)	$2,677.90 %of Total 100.00% ($2,677.90)	0.23
1. 1440x900	1,916 (11.88%)	1,492 (11.04%)	2,384 (12.29%)	37.54%	5.48	00:03:50	8 (17.78%)	$512.40 (19.13%)	0.5
2. 1920x1080	1,692 (10.49%)	1,499 (11.09%)	1,955 (10.08%)	51.87%	3.64	00:02:16	2 (4.44%)	$34.00 (1.27%)	0.1
3. 1680x1050	1,318 (8.17%)	924 (6.84%)	1,682 (8.67%)	26.93%	7.11	00:04:13	3 (6.67%)	$107.00 (4.00%)	0.1
4. 1366x768	1,205 (7.47%)	1,094 (8.10%)	1,441 (7.43%)	59.06%	2.89	00:02:17	0 (0.00%)	$0.00 (0.00%)	0.0
5. 2560x1440	1,186 (7.35%)	851 (6.30%)	1,428 (7.36%)	29.20%	5.75	00:03:09	0 (0.00%)	$0.00 (0.00%)	0.0
6. 1536x864	787 (4.88%)	681 (5.04%)	1,005 (5.18%)	50.95%	3.55	00:02:33	0 (0.00%)	$0.00 (0.00%)	0.0
7. 414x896	527 (3.27%)	496 (3.67%)	612 (3.16%)	45.10%	4.45	00:02:09	6 (13.33%)	$434.00 (16.21%)	0.9
8. 375x812	524 (3.25%)	484 (3.58%)	608 (3.13%)	41.45%	4.53	00:02:23	2 (4.44%)	$149.00 (5.56%)	0.5
9. 1280x720	514 (3.19%)	422 (3.12%)	654 (3.37%)	49.85%	4.31	00:03:24	0 (0.00%)	$0.00 (0.00%)	0.0

Figure 3.12: Google's top resolution report helps you explore what resolutions your users have their monitors set to so that you can make design decisions accordingly.

picture of how your users are interacting with your system. For Google Analytics it's called a "secondary dimension," and at the time this book was published, when looking at the "Screen Resolutions Report" you would need to set "Browser Size" as the secondary dimension so you can see the size at which users are actually seeing your system as compared to their device resolution as you can see in Figure 3.13.

This is important to understand because many times end users will have their browser set up to take only a portion of their screen. This could be because they are shopping at work and don't want their boss to see. It could be because their job requires them to use multiple applications at the same time so they divide their screen up into segments so they don't have to juggle windows all day. It doesn't really matter what the reason is, you just need to be aware that it is happening all the time for many reasons, and the result is that users are frequently working with systems designed for more screen space than they can actually dedicate to it. Because of this, some items go undiscovered and some interactions are harder to do or keep track of.

Once you have an understanding of the lowest common browser size that's being used regularly for your site or app, you can define where the fold is and begin designing for it.

You'll need to repeat that process for mobile as well. Depending on your specific case, you may need to do it for other device types also. Once you are done you'll have a much clearer picture of what users will see on any given page, and your system will perform better for both your users and your business because you took the time to account for the realities of your users' experience.

If you don't have the time to gather the data on this for your system, assume 1366×768 is where you should start for desktop/laptop usage. As of the date this book is published, that's a solid baseline that I've seen across many industries, and it's better to err on the conservative side with this sort of thing. As of early 2020 I validated this with landing pages from Apple, Google, and Amazon all coming in at this size or at the lower 960-pixel width.

If you can't get information on your system's mobile usage, use a service like www.browserstack.com. BrowserStack allows you to view your work on virtually any device for a small subscription fee and is very easy to work with. I'll discuss this in more detail in Chapter 4 in the section that covers "Testing across Platforms, Browsers, and Devices." Once you have the measurements that define what one screenful is for your system, you'll be ready to move on to the other aspects of composition.

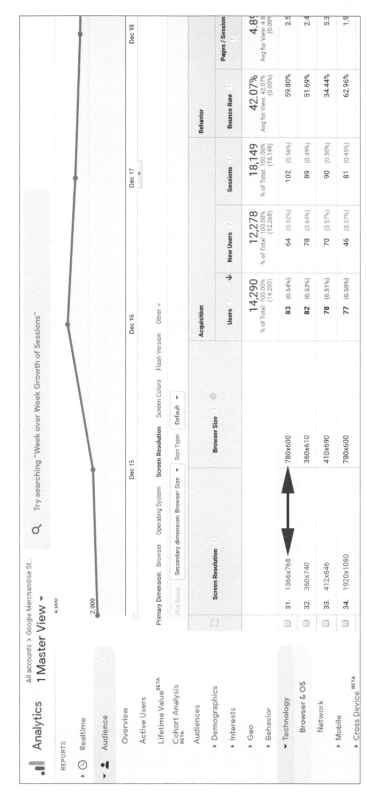

Figure 3.13: Resolution is only one part of the story. If users are using your system while at work they are likely to have multiple applications open and therefore may have the window in which your service is being displayed configured to be smaller than their full-screen resolution.

Scope

Once you know how much space you have to work with you'll need to know how to apply the information architecture you created previously to help your users as they complete their tasks.

Scope is one of the most important aspects of clearly communicating your information architecture. It is also an essential part of the visual hierarchy of any screen. What I mean by scope in this context is clearly defining the structure of the navigation and content in the design, and in doing so, ensuring that the relationships are clear to your users.

One area in which I see sites fail to clearly communicate scope within their interfaces is with their search functionality as is shown in Figure 3.14. If users see a search box at the top of the page above all other navigation, they will assume that the scope of the search will include the entire system. If they instead click one of the main navigation links and see a search box below the main navigation but very close to a data table, they will assume that the scope of that search is limited to the content of that table. In those examples it should be relatively easy for the user to guess what will happen.

The problem comes in when scope isn't accounted for properly. In the best case this will simply lead to a slight inconvenience if a user ends up navigating somewhere by mistake. One of the worst-case outcomes of scope confusion is when a user draws the wrong conclusion from the content or data that is being presented and makes decisions based on that misunderstanding.

To avoid confusion, always make sure that your visual hierarchy clearly illustrates the correct scoping relationships. Learning more about the following design principles will help you do that.

The Golden Triangle

The next crucial concept to understand when considering the composition is what's called "The Golden Triangle." The Golden Triangle is the triangle in the top left of your layout as shown in Figure 3.15. This is where a person's gaze naturally enters a composition, so it is important that crucial conversion content be placed there. The goal is to use the Golden Triangle as an entryway into the rest of your content, so make sure you are presenting something that will lead users in and encourage them to continue.

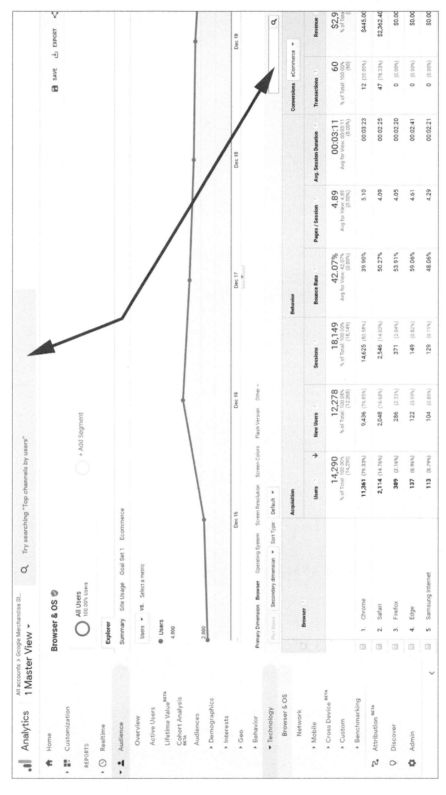

Figure 3.14: It is not always easy for users to comprehend the scope of a search box presented on the screen. Does this search check the entire system or is it set to only search part of the system?

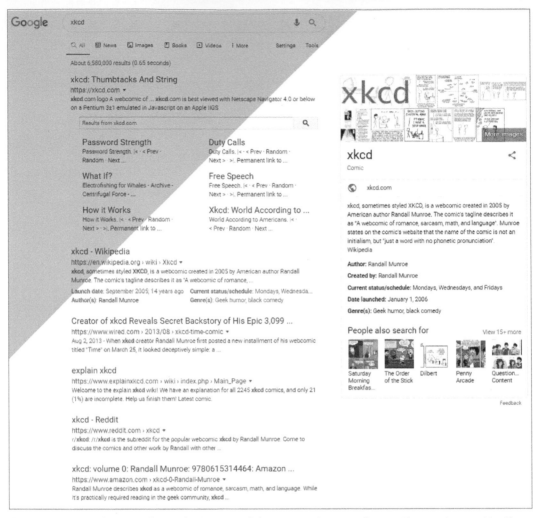

Figure 3.15: The Golden Triangle is the part of the screen that usually gets the most user attention.

The F, Z, and Other Gaze Patterns

Eye tracking studies have illustrated that there are common gaze patterns that people use when browsing content. The "F" pattern and "Z" pattern are closely related, and in general describe the flow of the user's gaze as it moves from the Golden Triangle to the right then shoots back across the page and anchors on the next element of high importance in the visual hierarchy on the left. From there the gaze moves back to the right either ingesting content or in search of it.

If you can picture how your eye moves back and forth over a page as you read, you can picture how these gaze patterns work as seen in the Heat Map in Figure 3.16. Because these patterns are deeply ingrained and widely recognized it is important to make sure you consider them as you create the composition of your page.

Figure 3.16: Heat Maps can show many useful trends when it comes to how the user's eye travels throughout your layout. One of the most common patterns is the F pattern illustrated in this figure.

Research by the Nielsen Norman Group has validated the concept that in cultures where users read right to left the patterns still exist, but they are flipped as you might expect.

These patterns are common because they represent users attempting to quickly parse the content of your pages looking for what is most relevant to them. These patterns are simply scanning strategies, and although you should be aware that they exist, they shouldn't be your ideal design goal. If your page is designed well with a strong visual hierarchy and content that is clear, concise, and appropriate for your user demographic, their gaze pattern will follow where you lead instead of the more generalized scanning patterns.

To be safe, make sure that the upper-left part of your layout contains the most impactful content so it will serve as an ambassador to lead the user into the rest of your content.

Gestalt Patterns

The Gestalt patterns tap into our brain's natural abilities for pattern recognition. Because these patterns are so strongly ingrained in our unconscious, they are also some of the most powerful techniques you can use to create compositions that clearly spacing between clustered subgroups, the proximity of those subgroups creates a supergroup.

That sounds more complex than it is. If you look back at Figure 3.19 now, you'll be able to see how the use of strategic spacing creates these visual groups and therefore makes it easier to use the interface.

Common region

Similar to proximity, designers can group things by creating visual regions in the layout and grouping items within those regions. Any element within a region is logically grouped in our minds because they share a well-defined visual space as illustrated in Figure 3.20.

Common Region

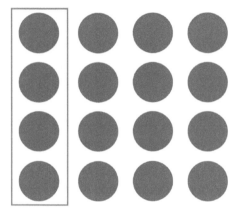

Figure 3.20: Common region defines part of the layout where items are visually grouped in order to distinguish them from other items in a layout.

Closure

In order to create a common region that is visually appealing in an interface, it's usually not going to be hard solid lines that act like a border. In cases where you want to create a common region, but you want to do it more subtly within the interface, you can leverage another Gestalt principle called closure. Closure is based on our brain's propensity to look for patterns and to complete incomplete shapes as seen in Figure 3.21. Closure can be used in the UI to minimize the amount of non-content elements that need to be used to promote the visual hierarchy thus improving the "data to ink" ratio that Tufte discussed in his book *The Visual Display of Quantitative Information*.

One way to use closure to create a common region in your interface would be to start with a box that represents the outer edge of your region and then remove lines from that

Closure

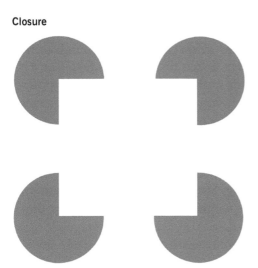

Figure 3.21: Closure is also commonly used in logo design to create imagery from disconnected shape groups, such as the square you can see in the middle of this figure.

box until you can no longer discern accurately what defines the region. Once there add some lines, or pieces of lines, back in until the region is recognizable again.

Continuity

Imagine that you have a great layout that starts off with a solid understanding of what size to design for based on user data. You moved on from there and put your highest-priority lead-in content into the upper left and you've used the grid and the Gestalt principles that we've discussed so far to their maximum effect. You've created a layout that clearly delineates the content into well-defined groups to improve scalability. If you have done all that, you are way ahead of the game, but there is more to do.

If you take it from there and apply a concept called continuity to your layout you'll be able to drive your user's gaze from point to point in your layout, helping users best understand your business proposition and complete their tasks faster.

Our perception of continuity is promoted by the part of our brain that seeks to track motion, so just like our brain is always looking to recognize patterns it's also looking to see and predict paths of motion. The search for continuity is so strong in our brains that it overrules the Gestalt principle of similarity in some cases.

Notice how in Figure 3.22 that even using color to create a strong sense of similarity doesn't override your brain's initial desire to see the items on the horizontal line as belonging to the same group and the items on the curved line as being in their own separate group.

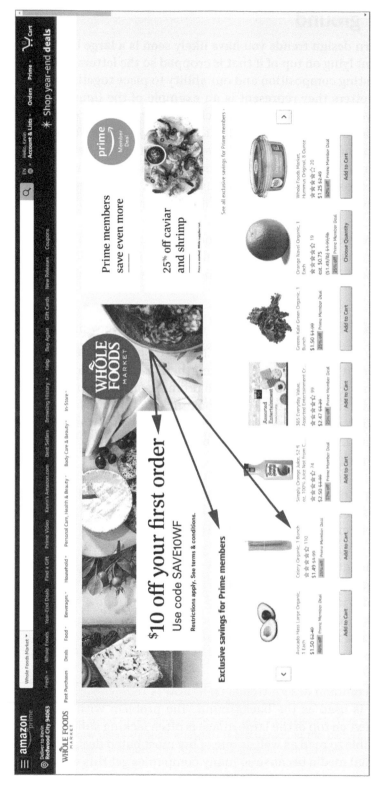

Figure 3.24: Scale is one more way to help establish hierarchy in your layout.

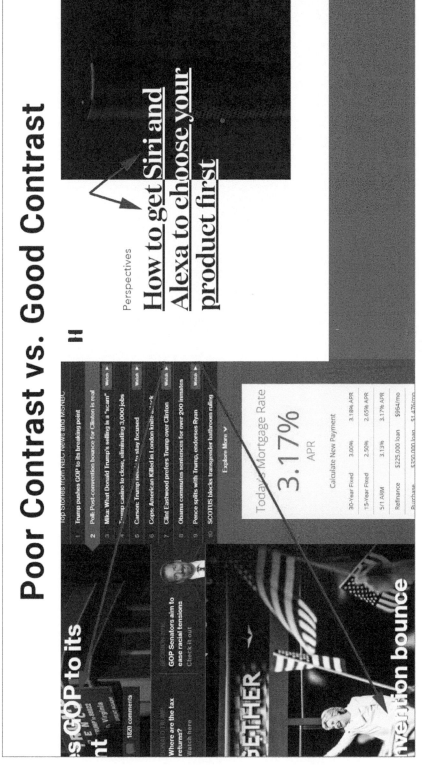

Figure 3.25: Contrast is one of the most important aspects of making sure your design is readable. If your site has insufficient contrast, users may still be able to complete their tasks, but the experience won't be as good as it should be.

Color

Once you have a layout that users can easily scan, read, and comprehend without the use of color as seen in Figure 3.26, it is safe to add color. I recognize that most in the design industry do not work this way, but I'm stating it here because if content is designed this way it will be much more likely to be accessible to those with disabilities. In addition, there are strong ethical, legal, and financial reasons that accessibility should be an important part of your design process.

Figure 3.26: Starting your design work off in grayscale will help ensure that your final full-color result is accessible to users with disabilities by forcing you to create a visual hierarchy that doesn't rely on color.

I'm not going to go into the details of selecting colors that are pleasing here because that could be (and is) a book in itself. Others have covered the topic much better than I ever will. *Color: A Workshop for Artists and Designers* would be a great book to read if you want to learn to use color well.

What I do want to make sure you know is that color doesn't just support your brand. It impacts the usability by being another design element that impacts the visual hierarchy of your design. If you created the grayscale version of your design and your hierarchy is working, you should then start going back over your design and applying the colors that are necessary to support your brand by applying them one by one at the same relative value as the grayscale value that they are replacing as seen in Figure 3.27.

Figure 3.27: This full-color exploration shows that your design can have enough contrast and be accessible while still missing some key elements that need to be considered. In this case the color choices do not support the brand very well.

That's the first step in the process. You are likely going to need to revisit the value and intensity of your colors, and even sometimes change the hue altogether to create a balanced design that represents your brand well and supports users as they scan the page.

Thematic Appropriateness

Although the design in Figure 3.27 works from a visual hierarchy and contrast point of view, it's not a great fit from a thematic appropriateness point of view. If this site was selling Easter eggs it might be a great fit, but since they are a UX design agency they would likely want a color scheme that is more conservative and isn't such a big departure from their current branding like what is shown in Figure 3.28.

Color is just one aspect of thematic appropriateness. The use of images, videos, fonts, writing style, shapes of various elements, interaction styles, and spacing can all be used to improve how the design of your system communicates the intended branding or themes.

It's pretty obvious that if you are creating an interface that helps a military pilot navigate, you are going to want to focus on barebones aesthetics that support the intended use without cluttering the interface as is illustrated in Figure 3.29. Cluttering the design with branding, or worse yet, distracting visual elements that may take attention away from important information can cause disastrous results.

On the other hand, if you were creating a video game that simulates air combat in an A-10 it might make perfect sense to use elements of the actual A-10 interface in your game navigation menus so that users stay immersed in the experience while they are interacting with the game configuration settings.

In Figure 3.30 you'll see that the grayscale interface with a very dark background with almost white text creates strong contrast and improves readability, and very closely matches the interface of the Tactical Display in Figure 3.29.

Imagine if the interface in Figure 3.30 used bright pastel colors like those used in Figure 3.27. Although the design would still be useful and usable, the lack of thematic appropriateness would negatively impact the experience. With that in mind, it's not hard to imagine how font choices, buttons styles and shapes, sounds, etc., can all be used to either support or detract from the aesthetic of your design and how well it supports the overall experience.

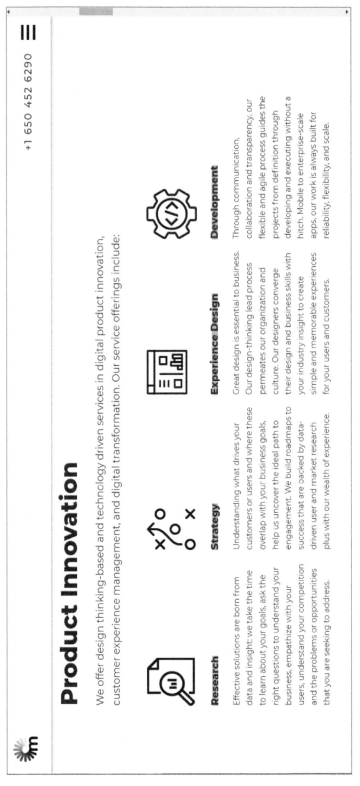

Figure 3.28: The existing version of the site is much more conservative. There isn't much color used but what they do use highlights the selected content to promote scannability.

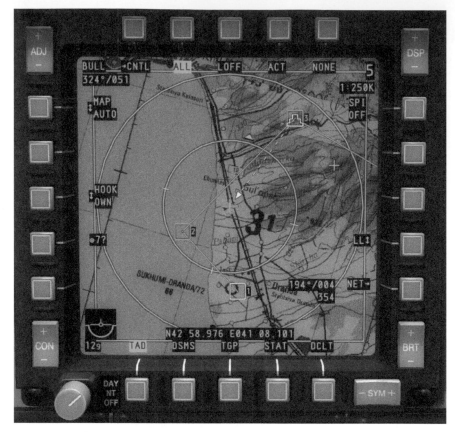

Figure 3.29: 60 A-10C Warthog Tactical Awareness Display
www.digitalcombatsimulator.com/en/products/warthog.

Data Visualization

The military pilot example is an extreme case because life-and-death decisions are made using what the pilot understands based on that tactical display, but it helps illustrate that data visualization in general is probably the aspect of the design profession that is most likely to impact life-or-death decisions. This is true not only in the military, but also in fields as diverse as healthcare and policy making.

Most times people who make critical decisions based on data are not looking at the raw data itself. Generally those who are trying to make decisions are looking at a visualization that has been designed to help simplify, summarize, and prioritize the information that can be derived from the raw data. This abstraction from the raw data puts the viewers in a position where they need to carefully observe what is being presented and critically think about how it's being communicated so that they are not misled.

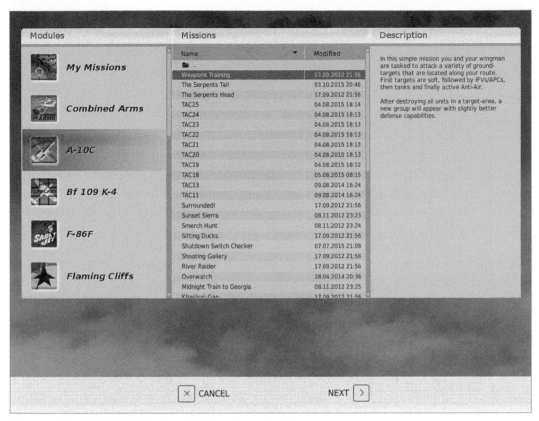

Figure 3.30: DCS A-10C Warthog Mission Selection Menu
www.digitalcombatsimulator.com/en/products/warthog.

There are many books that cover this topic in-depth. Some of the most respected designers in the world have tackled this topic far better than I ever could, so instead of trying to top them what I want to do is help you understand the core issues when it comes to the user experience of data visualization, make you aware of some of the challenges, and hopefully inspire you to dig in and learn as much as you can from the masters such as Tufte.

First, a little inspiration. Data today is what crude oil was to the Rockefellers. Data is hugely valuable and is the foundation of the wealth that companies like Google, Amazon, and Facebook have managed to amass over the past couple decades. What I'm saying here is that if you want to have a career outlook that is looking great for the foreseeable future, make sure you are doing something related to helping businesses leverage data.

To reiterate, data is like the crude oil that made previous generations incredibly wealthy, and information is its refined product. Information is what we all consume and what businesses use to make decisions that make or break their bottom line.

The data maturity model looks like this:

1. First you have *data*
2. Then you do some analysis on the data and create some *information*
3. From that information you can further refine it and derive some *observations*
4. Finally, with all the previous steps achieved you can move on to making *recommendations*

If you haven't spent a lot of time thinking about data this way, this may all still feel a bit abstract. To help bring it into the real world, let's consider a patient who goes to the doctor. The doctor takes in some *data* like height, weight, blood pressure, etc. When looking at the patient's height and weight, he shares some *information* derived from that data with the patient. The information the doctor shares is the patient's body mass index, or BMI. When the doctor combines that information with the blood pressure data he can share an *observation* that the high blood pressure number is likely linked to the high BMI number. From there the doctor would combine what he knows about that observation with his previous medical knowledge and make a *recommendation* for the patient to lose some weight in order to lower her BMI and hopefully blood pressure as well.

This process works very well when all the instruments are performing as expected and the doctor has the required training/skill to make the observations and recommendations. Many times in real-world situations this process is complicated by factors such as inaccurate data, biases impacting analysis and the information that is derived from it, missed observations, and recommendations that have been ill informed by errors in the previous steps.

If you are responsible for the user experience of a system that presents data to users, your first and most important responsibility is to work with the teams that gather the data and validate that the data is accurate. If you have bad data, you have no shot of having good information, observations, or recommendations, so start there and stay vigilant. You can't just check once and assume from there that it's OK from then on.

Once you have confidence that the data is correct, test out how it's being analyzed to create information. Ask those responsible to explain how they do what they do. My experience working with researchers and data scientists is that they will most often be excited to share what they do and how their information is derived. If they are not excited to share, that should be a cause for concern.

To be clear, you don't have to understand everything they say or how each value is calculated. That's their job, and validating their work is the responsibility of their teams and the business owners. You should walk out of those conversations feeling confident that your questions have been answered and that the values you are incorporating into your experiences are accurate. If that isn't the case, then you should continue to dig into whatever the discrepancies are until you have confidence in what you are being given to work with.

In many ways designing a data visualization is exactly like any other design challenge you'll face. It's all about communication. Keep these items in mind as you design your visualization:

- Knowing exactly what story you are trying to tell is the first step. If you are trying to tell the story of how gas prices influence consumer confidence, you should be able to state that clearly before you begin.

- Choose the best data visualization type to communicate the story. Doing a web search on "choosing the best data visualization" will provide you with some tools that will help with your decision. If you are new to all of this, experiment with a few variations to get a sense for the strengths and weaknesses of each type for telling the type of story you are trying to communicate.

  Microsoft Excel and similar tools have built-in previews that will allow you to explore the various types of visualizations there are to choose from.

- Use all the elements of design that we discussed previously to create a visual hierarchy that allows the user to scan, read, and accurately comprehend the story you are telling.

- When you are done with that, look back on what you have created and remove anything you can from the visualization that doesn't detract from the user's ability to comprehend it.

- If this is a visualization that will be updated with new data periodically, you'll want to test it with a range of data so that you can see if your design holds up over the range of values you are likely to encounter. It's always good to design how your visualizations will look if the data fails to load, how it will look in an ideal case, and how it will look if your values are at the extremes of what's possible so that you have considered all of that and so the developers will know what to do in those cases.

- Test your visualizations on users that match your target demographic. I know from personal experience that I tend to create visualizations that are too dense (have too many types of data in them) because I love a visualization that tells an interesting and complex story. Most people do not. Many people I've tested with are looking for an interesting simple story that they can comprehend quickly and share with others. It's a good habit in the UX field to stay humble and check in with your target users when you can.

Further Reading

LinkedIn Learning

www.linkedin.com/learning/graphic-design-foundations-layout-and-composi-
   tion/welcome

Udemy Graphic Design Theory

www.udemy.com/course/graphic-design-theory-for-beginners-course

AIGA–The Professional Association for Design

www.aiga.org/design

CH 4

MAKE IT FUNCTIONAL

"Our highest priority is to satisfy the customer through early and continuous delivery of valuable software."

—The Agile Manifesto

This chapter won't teach you to be a developer. It will teach you how to evaluate code from a user experience point of view and provide you with further reading if you want to learn more about how to be a UX-focused developer.

If you are a designer or a person in the product organization at your company, your relationship with the performance of the services that you design might be as simple as "it works" or "it doesn't work." When I say performance in this context, I'm not talking about how well the system is delivering on your Key Performance Indicators (KPIs). In this case, I'm talking about how well your service is running. How well your service is running will often have a large impact on your KPIs. In other words, if your checkout process is offline (poor performance), your conversation rate (KPI) will drop to 0% during that outage.

If you take anything away from reading this chapter, let it be that it doesn't matter if you have the most amazing content designed by the very best designer if your users can't see it because the page doesn't load or takes too long to load—that's a terrible user experience.

This type of performance is usually measured at the highest level by monitoring the following:

Availability
The percent of the time the system is up and running so users can interact successfully with it.

Response Time and Latency
The amount of time it takes for the system to react to the user interaction and send the appropriate response.

Error Rates
The percent of interactions that include some sort of system error.

My experience working with companies that range in size from the very biggest in the world down to brand-new startups is that most people in the organization do not understand how important the performance of a system is to the user experience. When you consider that Pinterest increased signups by 15% by reducing perceived wait times by 40%[1] and the BBC found that they lost an additional 10% of users for every additional second their site took to load, it's easy to see that performance should be taken seriously when designing your experiences.[1]

To help teams understand how their site is performing and how that performance might be impacting their bottom-line, Google has created some tools[2] that illustrate the impact and provide recommendations on how to improve as seen in Figure 4.1.

Tools like this can be helpful in framing the problem, but having your own analytics set up to monitor how successful users are at completing key tasks, and how well your systems are performing, will provide a great foundation for your team. We will discuss analytics in more detail in the next chapter, but for now it's important to understand that you can and should be aware of not only how your users are interacting with your system, but also how your system is performing for your users.

As a product team member or UX professional there isn't much you are going to do directly to impact the availability of your system. There are other teams of professionals that are making the decisions in terms of how the system gets developed and deployed. In my experience, the best way to push to have performance considered a top priority and gain some leverage within your business is to tie the performance to dollars if possible.

I was able to do that at an ecommerce company I worked with by keeping track of the times and dates of deployments. I suspected that the deployments that were being done during business hours were very bad for users and our conversion rate, but no one had ever looked into it. Once I had the dates and times mapped, I used their analytics tools to look for signs that the experience was being impacted.

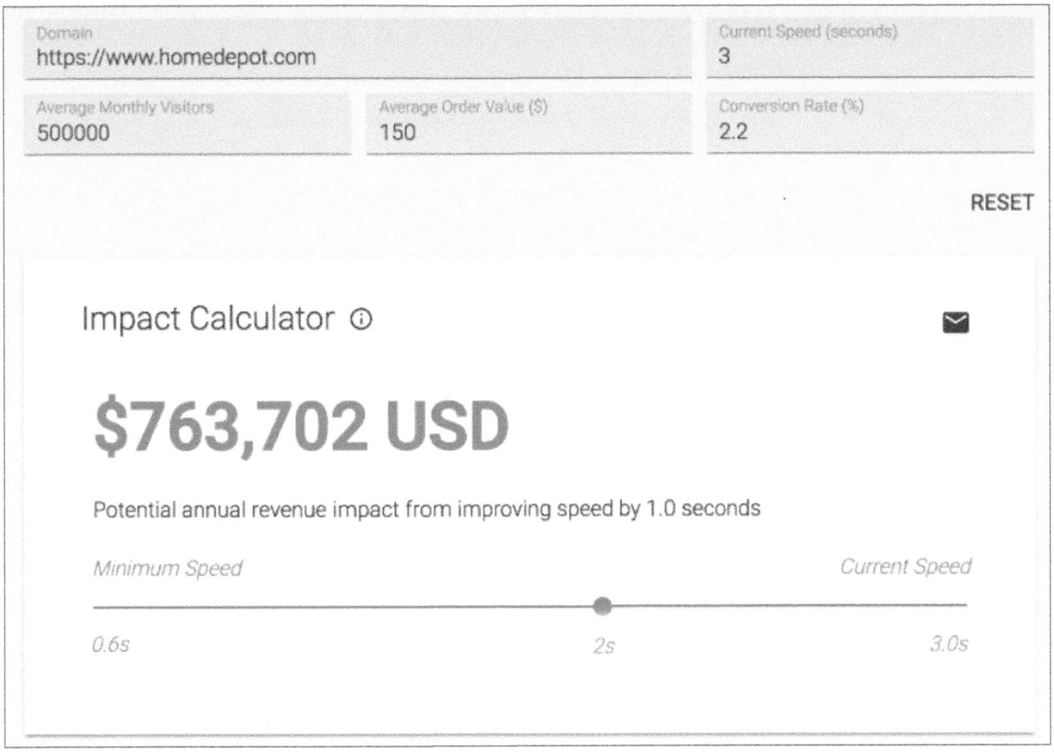

Figure 4.1: Performance impact calculators like this may not be perfect, but they help to frame the performance conversation around real-world business outcomes and that helps teams prioritize their efforts.

It was very easy to see that the "time to serve pages" had been dramatically impacted and it was also easy to see that the servers reported a lot of "500" (server) errors while the deployments were happening. In the end, I was able to estimate that each deployment was costing more than $10,000 in lost sales.

The business changed its practices based on this information and now only deploys during what we identified as being the lowest traffic time slots. They were also able to justify investing in modernizing their processes for deployments so that they could virtually eliminate the "500" errors. It only took a day or so to do the research that identified the issues. These types of changes aren't as "sexy" as a site redesign or new feature that gets promoted at tradeshows, but they can oftentimes have more impact on the user experience and your bottom line at a fraction of the cost or effort.

Aside from deployment and general stability type issues, there are a few other key elements of how your service is developed that you should be aware of so that you can monitor and provide feedback as issues arise. What I'm about to present is normally considered exclusively the domain of the development team, but don't let that stop you from learning some new skills and taking more control over how your work ends up being presented to users.

Framework-itis and Code Bloat

One of the biggest issues that I see currently is what I call *framework-itis*. A framework can be thought of as a system of "canned" code that can be used by development teams to speed up the development process, help improve consistency and reliability, and provide a certain amount of predictability to the development process. That all sounds great, right? Why wouldn't you want to do this?

Frameworks have many valid and valuable benefits, but those can be outweighed if the team doesn't use them properly or relies on them too much. When I started coding websites in the mid-1990s, the standard we worked toward was that the entire page had to be able to be transferred to the user within 25 kilobytes. That included all the content, images, logos, and HTML markup necessary to render the page. That standard is all but completely obsolete here in the United States, but it doesn't mean that you shouldn't try to reasonably minimize the amount you require your users to download, especially if you plan to have a global audience.

The following are the download sizes of some of the world's biggest brands:

- **Google:**   20 kilobytes
- **Microsoft:**   851 kilobytes
- **Apple:**   1.6 megabytes
- **Amazon:**   4.4 megabytes

Notice that Google's home page is *much* smaller than the rest. They have always had a strong focus on efficiency, and they recommend and promote efficiency via their algorithms. With Google's "Next Billion Users" initiative, they are going to need to serve even more users in the farthest reaches of the world, on the slowest connections, on the weakest devices, to users who could have any disability. It's a big challenge, and core elements of that effort to create great experiences are going to be flexibility and efficiency within the code that powers them.[3]

Your team most likely doesn't need to go to the extremes that Google does, but they should take care not to fall into some of the common pitfalls of using frameworks. The biggest issues I encounter are:

- A poorly chosen framework that creates artificial limitations on what can be done within the solution you are developing. I've been told by development teams countless times that they cannot implement the design that the product team researched, designed, and validated with users. Many times the reason they give is that it won't be easy to get it to work within the framework they are stuck using now.

- It's important to note that the UX teams should be aware of what frameworks are being used and how those frameworks impact what is available to them as well. There has to be mutual respect between teams and a willingness to be flexible within limits. That being said, when Steve Jobs was working on developing the iPhone his team didn't look at an existing mobile phone and use it as a template to build their new phone because that would have been the easiest path. The Apple team designed novel solutions to problems users didn't even know they had and built those solutions using novel technology. That is the hard way for sure, but if you have a valuable business challenge that requires a novel solution, trying to shoehorn it into an existing framework might artificially limit your potential for success.

- A required update to the newest version of the framework breaks existing functionality in ways that no one expected and no one caught before it went live. The evil twin of this issue is when updating one framework conflicts with other frameworks you are using in ways your team wasn't expecting, so now the push to create an emergency fix is pushing out other UX initiatives.

- Your code becomes so bloated by adding a large framework to your codebase just to solve one small problem causing the experience to become noticeably less responsive.

Those are some of the key issues that I run into, but it's important to consider that there is an opportunity cost to using frameworks as well. If your team becomes too reliant on a framework it can kill innovation conversations at the product level before they even get fully explored from a business-value point of view. As the old saying goes, if you have a hammer, you need to make sure you aren't only able to solve problems that involve nails.

Testing across Platforms, Browsers, and Devices

OK, so your team has designed and built something that is ready to launch. Have you tested it on the devices it is likely to be used on, at the resolutions it's likely to be used within, and in the environments your solution will be used in? If not, don't worry—you are not alone. Sadly, I see this all the time. Often companies ask me to work with them because they see a problem in their conversion rate but they don't know what to do to fix it. Many times, they try offering lower prices or some sort of bundle. Nothing seems to resolve their conversion issue. It's not until I complete my first usability testing session that we start to see how elements of the system are hurting the conversion rate more than anything product related.

So how do you go about testing across a wide range of devices if you are a small team of just a couple founders, or a large team of designers and developers? There isn't anything better than testing on real devices, but that's not always practical. I've certainly worked with companies that have an entire QA lab setup with many devices of all types set up and ready to be used for testing, but in my 20+ years a lab like that is the exception instead of the rule.

I've found that a much more realistic option is a subscription to BrowserStack (www .browserstack.com) as shown in figure 4.2. For $30 per month you can have access to virtually any device/resolution combination you could possibly need. It's very simple to interact with, and in my experience speeds up the validation process tremendously. For $100 per month a team of five can have access and you don't need to maintain that cost while you aren't using it. I sign up for a few months while it's super relevant to the work I'm doing and then take a few months off while I'm more focused on other types of work.

Figure 4.2: This figure illustrates how comprehensive the BrowserStack device selection is.

You would need to either use your analytics to monitor your usage and determine what resolutions and devices you need to test, or take your best guess based on what you know of the market. That second option is OK at the very beginning of a startup, but you really should get your analytics set up so you can make a decision based on data versus guessing.

Once you have your target devices and resolutions identified, you would need to log in to BrowserStack and set up those devices so you can use them to test as shown in Figure 4.3.

From there, all you need to do is enter the URL that you want to test and within a few seconds you'll be looking at a screen that shows exactly how that device type and resolution will look in on a wide range of devices as is illustrated in Figure 4.4. BrowserStack is the fastest, easiest, and cheapest way I know of to verify that your systems are working well everywhere you expect them to.

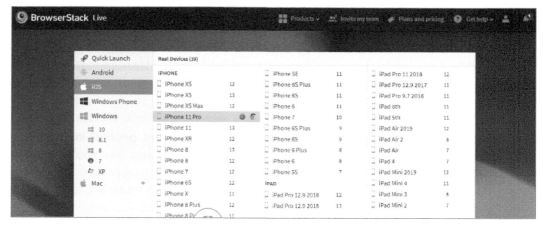

Figure 4.3: The interface allows users to select what OS and device combination they would like to test on. I haven't run into a case yet where BrowserStack didn't have what I needed to test my work.

Figure 4.4: Being able to see what your work looks on virtually any device almost instantaneously is incredibly valuable. It wasn't long ago that design firms had to maintain actual devices onsite to be able to test like this.

Now that you have seen how the testing process works, let's revisit the process of determining what devices and screen sizes to test in the first place.

If you have an analytics package set up or other method of tracking usage, then you should be able to identify the devices that are accessing your systems most frequently. I would caution, though, that you need to consider that your usage might currently be a self-fulfilling prophecy. I've had clients say to me that they don't need to support mobile devices because, according to their analytics, not many people are accessing the system using them. Sometimes that is actually true. Other times the reason that no one is using a system on their mobile device is because the experience is so terrible that they don't want to use it. There is obviously a big difference between those two things, so if you

Visual Hierarchy and Data Visualization

The importance of visual hierarchy has already been discussed, but it is important to remember that it is essential that your design does not require color to communicate the hierarchy. Color is a great way to enhance and promote the hierarchical structure, but it cannot be an essential part or the design will not be accessible to as many people as it should be.

Another important concept to remember is that status indicators and data visualizations need to use both shape and color to represent the status. A text description is ideal as well if there is room, along with a key explaining how the colors and shapes relate to the data.

Zooming and Dynamic Layouts

Some users will need to zoom in on your content even if you have already designed it to be readable by most users. Your system will need to be designed so that users can zoom in to at least 200% as shown in Figure 4.5 and still be able to access and use the system controls. To do that, your team will need to develop it with flexible containers to create what is known as a "fluid" layout. This process also aids in creating responsive layouts, so you'll get dual benefit from the effort.

Figure 4.5: Example of a zoomed-in fluid layout

Line Length

There are things we can do as designers and developers that help make the experience feel more effortless. Using font sizes that are large enough to be read without straining is one of those things that gets talked about a lot. Line length doesn't get talked about often, but it is very important as well.

You should strive to keep your line lengths below 80 characters because more than that requires excessive eye travel. This type of thing can be a minor inconvenience for some users and for others it can seriously impact their ability to scan, read, and comprehend the content. There is a reason books have been formatted in similar ways for the past 2,000 years, and there is no reason to throw out all that expertise now just because we are displaying text on screens.

Keyboard Shortcuts

All interactions that are possible in your system should also be possible using only a keyboard. Keyboard shortcuts and alternative interactions are the best way to ensure that disabled users can fully interact with your system. This also includes being able to stop automatic animations or content transitions so that the user has control over when the next piece of content is presented. I'm not disabled in any way, but I find it very frustrating when automatic carousel-type presentations remove content from view before I am done reading it. That problem is compounded if your user is disabled.

These are just the highlights. In order to create a truly accessible experience you will need to consider how all elements of the Section 508 / Web Content Accessibility Guidelines apply to your system and then take the steps necessary to implement the recommendations. This might sound difficult, but I assure you that once your teams are familiar with what needs to be done, it becomes part of their everyday process and your users' experience will benefit from it.

Further Reading

There is a lot to cover in this topic and I hope that what I've written so far has helped to drive some interest. Maybe you aren't the person on the team who needs to do a deep dive on the subject, but it's likely that your role as a person pushing to improve the user experience puts you in the best position to advocate for and promote this type of continued learning within your teams. The following are some more comprehensive resources that may be useful as you continue your journey:

Mismatch: How Inclusion Shapes Design

www.amazon.com/Mismatch-Inclusion-Simplicity-Technology-Business/dp/0262038889

An Introduction to web accessibility

www.w3.org/WAI/fundamentals/accessibility-intro

measured. There is a slight conflict of interest there but in most cases, good people doing good work understand that it's better to fail and iterate intelligently than to hide the failure behind false numbers. If you question what I just said, please consider that many people in the company you work for are dedicating their life to investing in, designing, building, marketing, and supporting the work that the team is doing. They are doing that with the blind faith that everyone is being open and honest about where the efforts are succeeding and where they are failing so that the leaders have the best information possible to make their decisions. Lying in cases like this has negative consequences that ripple throughout entire communities.

If a product leader in an organization wants to convince the board of directors to invest millions of dollars in the development of her idea, it can become tempting to "fudge the numbers." The easiest way to do that is to simply change the numbers in a research report to make them tell the story that is most beneficial to her position. That's also the easiest way to get caught, because oftentimes something gets missed while the numbers are being changed and an eagle-eyed reviewer might spot inconsistencies that call the findings of the entire report into question. The people I've encountered who were interested in committing this kind of fraud were not stupid people, so their plan wasn't to rig the numbers. Their plan was to rig the process for collecting the numbers, and that is where their path crossed with mine.

The worst case of this I ever encountered was at a very large company that I'm sure most everyone has heard of. I was asked to work with them to explore and document customer sentiment in relation to a new product idea in which they were considering investing many millions of dollars. The process started off well, with me interviewing participants in a recording studio so that the product team would have great footage of our findings to use in the report. Things started to go poorly when it became clear that many participants didn't find all that much value in the service that was being demonstrated. In general, the perception was that the service might be useful, but most didn't see enough value to pay anything for it.

Under normal circumstances, that is a perfectly valid finding and one that the team would be thrilled to understand before investing millions of dollars and years of time into developing something no one really wanted. With that in mind, teams would normally either run another study with new participants to see if maybe the idea was still a good one but only for another demographic, or they might take the feedback and tweak the idea to see if they could modify it in a way that would generate the value that was missing in this round of testing.

Either of those are healthy responses to test results that don't go as you might have hoped. What happened instead was that I was called into an impromptu meeting between testing sessions where the team discussed what was going on and how the results were not telling the desired story. I pointed out that maybe we had the wrong demographic or that maybe the concept could be tweaked, but overall my opinion was that we should finish the testing without making changes. That way, we would have a complete and valid set of findings to report on and could make those adjustments after reviewing with the broader team, including leadership.

The person leading the research effort from the product team told me that what we were gathering up to that point was unacceptable and that he wanted to make changes to the script to get "better" information. Making adjustments to a testing process during the actual testing is not entirely unheard of, but it's not a great practice for many reasons. In this case, it went from being a bad process to fraud when he further elaborated that I would need to wear an earpiece in the following sessions and ask the specific questions he wanted to be answered based on what the participants were saying as I interviewed them.

This was an odd request, but I didn't recognize that this person was fundamentally trying to rig the results. At first, I thought he thought I wasn't doing my job well and wanted to exert more control over the process. I'm open to criticism and ready to learn a better way of doing things, so I agreed to give it a try and we kicked things off with the next participant.

After reviewing the basic functionality and value proposition I began to ask probing questions about the participant's perceptions. This is when I started getting specific questions coming in via the earpiece. The first thing I was asked to pass along to the participant was "Tell me more about what you like about this service." This was followed up by "Please tell me why you feel this service is worth $2.99 per month."

For the first question, the participant was easily able to list items he liked about the service but stumbled a bit with the second question, starting off with "Well, to be honest, I'm not sure I would want to pay for this, but I guess maybe having feature X might be helpful. . . I'm not sure." In my earpiece, I heard the product leader say "Great, we can cut out that other stuff. That part where they mention feature X will make a great sound bite so that's the sort of thing we are looking for going forward."

If you don't immediately see the problem here that's OK, but it's also why I wrote this part of the book. I wanted to make it very clear that what had just transpired in that session crossed the line so you'll be aware of these types of things if you encounter them.

First, changing the process in the middle of a test is usually a bad idea because it means that not all participants were tested on the same information using the same process and, therefore, you are no longer comparing apples to apples when doing the analysis and reporting. Misleading and inconsistent results are pretty much guaranteed.

Like I mentioned earlier, it is not unheard of to change things up mid-session, but it's best to note that you are going to need more participants to make up for the ones you worked with before the changes and that you likely had a flaw in your test preparation if you needed to make this change in the first place.

The second prompt, "Please tell me why you feel this service is worth $2.99 per month," is a terrible prompt because it leads the participants. It's a lot like asking "Washington, great president or greatest president?" It's pretty easy to see that you just boxed their responses into saying that Washington is great *or* that they'll be put in the uncomfortable position of saying something like "Well, he certainly isn't the greatest president" only to then have the corrupt person running the session mark the participant's response as "great president" because the participant didn't say "greatest" specifically.

In the case of the session I was facilitating, the person writing the report could say something like "When answering the question 'Why do you feel this service is worth $2.99 per month?' 10 out of 10 participants mentioned feature X." Since we already know that most participants said they wouldn't pay for it in the first place, it is easy to see that this is a misleading statement. A board of directors getting a presentation on the findings would assume that along with mentioning feature X, the participants had previously agreed that they would pay $2.99 a month, and that is a terrible assumption promoted by a product leader using the research process to commit fraud.

Once I recognized that I was hired to be the expert stamp of approval on the story they wanted to tell, I removed myself from the process.

This is just one example of how it can happen. Please be aware that it can happen, it's not always obvious that it is happening, and you should do your best to not take part in or promote this type of misleading behavior. Remember what I said at the beginning of the book about our work in UX having the potential to save life—not necessarily save lives, but "life"? This is a great example of wasting life, and I hope you don't want any part of it.

Analytics

Don't skip this section of the book!

I understand that many of you might come from a design-heavy background and may feel intimidated by the idea of incorporating analytics into your process, but this section of the book is all about helping you see the value and get over any fear you might have. If you don't know how your solutions are performing in the real world, how will you ever know how to approach your iterations? You might say, "Well, I have a team that does that," and that's a wonderful thing if they are doing their job well, but I encourage you to apply your critical thinking skills whenever presented with information about how your systems are performing. You'll be amazed at how many times just a little bit of review with a critical eye uncovers issues that might mislead your business decisions.

One example of this sort of issue occurred when I was working with one of the largest privately owned companies in the United States. I asked the analytics team for a report on system usage over the previous quarter because I wanted to confirm some numbers I heard the Director of Product state in a meeting. The numbers seemed odd to me, so I wanted to check them.

After about a week, I received the report from the analytics department and saw that the numbers were different from what the Director had stated, but they were larger than I expected. I decided that I would log in to the analytics tool our team used at the time to see if I could learn more, and it wasn't long before I spotted the issue. The numbers the analytics team gave me included usage from each of our offices spread out around the country, as well as our actual usage from paying customers. This was easy to see because the cities with the highest usage were also cities where we had offices. Once our internal traffic was excluded, the numbers roughly aligned with what the Director had reported, so I moved on to other tasks. If I didn't take the time to validate what was handed to me I likely would have had an embarrassing conversation with the Director that ended with me looking foolish.

In a previous chapter, we reviewed the basic process for testing with users. That method of testing is qualitative, and overall the method is a wonderful approach to use if you know what you want to test. If you don't really know what to test or what you are looking for, it can be time-consuming and expensive without providing much value.

This is where usage analytics shines. As a quantitative process it is great at describing *what* is going on, and if you know that you can accurately describe what is working well and what is not. Once you know what's not working, you know where to put your focus when you move to your next iteration.

I can't cover how all the analytics packages on the market work in detail, but what I can do is get you up to speed on what you'll need your analytics package to do and why. With that information, you can either work to set up your analytics to provide the information you need, or ask your team to report on those things for you. It doesn't really matter how you get the information as long as you have it.

Conversions and Micro Conversions

If you have worked with analytics at all you have likely heard of conversion funnels. In the traditional ecommerce example, a typical conversion funnel would look something like what is shown in Table 5.1.

It's called a funnel because the numbers are larger at the top and get smaller as you progress toward the bottom. At the end of this conversion funnel, we can see that this example site has a conversion rate of 5%.

Table 5.1 A Typical Conversion Funnel Example

Number of Users Who	Number of Users
Visited the landing page	100
Clicked to a gallery page	80
Clicked on a product detail page	60
Added a product to their cart	50
Entered the checkout process	40
Entered their address	20
Entered their credit card information	10
Reached the confirmation page	5

Micro Conversions

It's important to consider each step and what might be causing users to leave the funnel at that stage. As part of the process, you should consider micro conversion. A micro conversion is the measure of an individual step in the journey that users take on their way to completing your overall conversion goal.

Each step listed in Table 5.1 could be considered a micro conversion, but those are not the only ones. You'll need to identify and track the conversions and micro conversions that matter for your specific system. In the case of an ecommerce site, it would be helpful to consider the number of visits that included usage of the search functionality. For this example, we'll say that 45% of users used search. With that information, you should be curious to learn how their overall conversion compares to users who did not use search. To do that, you would narrow your focus and create a report that includes only traffic from users who used the search functionality as part of their purchase process. I can't tell you how to do that within your specific tool, but know that you should be able to do it (or your team should) and that this type of drilling in is essential in uncovering insights that will help you refine your user experience. For the sake of this example, let's say that you discover that their conversion rate is 15%. That is a full 10% higher than the conversion rate for users who did not use search in their purchase process.

With that knowledge, a reasonable plan might be to design a user journey that promotes the search functionality and test to see if it has a positive impact on your overall conversion rate.

Creating Conversion Funnels to Measure Success

You can and should create your own conversion flows regardless of the type of system you are working on. The system I'm currently working on has a number of micro conversion that culminate in a final conversion of receiving a notification when something changes in a file that the user is monitoring.

One of the micro conversion is clicking the main call to action on the landing page to kick off the process. From there, another would be when the user completes the initial sign-up process. Next, a user would need to select some files to monitor. That's another micro conversion. Each of these examples becomes a line item on the path to completing the larger conversion goal.

Not all conversions will directly put money in the bank. Many self-help and support conversions might help with engagement or retention, which are sometimes hard to tie back to exact dollars. This doesn't mean they are not valuable to your team or that they should be ignored.

One challenge many face once they start tracking conversions is not knowing what a good conversion rate would be for whatever they are measuring. In some cases, you can Google information like this, but in others, you won't be able to find much guidance. In that case, just create an internal benchmark and work to improve on what you already have.

Your internal benchmarks will usually become more and more accurate over time. If you can associate outside influences with your benchmarks, you'll better understand how they are impacting your numbers. If you imagine you had a web page that sold convertible cars it might be common sense that the conversion rate would be higher in the spring and summer vs. the fall and winter. This is one of the main reasons so many companies rely on Year Over Year (YoY) numbers instead of just looking at how they are doing compared to last month. There are likely similar things within your business cycle that would impact your numbers and being aware of them can help you communicate and plan for what to expect.

Be Curious and Analytical

Previously in this chapter, I mentioned that I didn't trust some numbers that the Director of Product had stated and then that I didn't trust the numbers that the analytics team gave me to help validate the original numbers. It's safe to say that I have trust issues when it comes to usage analytics, and I think that is very healthy because that lack of trust is the foundation of what drives me to think analytically about the usage of the experiences I help create. I highly recommend that you get in the habit of questioning any numbers that you are presented with and if you find a reason to doubt them, politely discuss those concerns with those who created the presentation.

To continue with our example, I'll say that in my experience many teams would be happy to know that their overall conversion rate is 5%. I wouldn't be as happy, because 5% is about double the average conversion rate in the United States for an ecommerce site, and although it is entirely possible that 5% might be accurate, I would want to validate that before I felt good about it. It's not hard to identify industry benchmarks like what I just described as the global average U.S. conversion rate. A simple Google search should point you in the right direction, and having this sort of benchmark information is helpful when trying to create a complete picture of the health of your system.

When I suspect a number I'm looking at is false, I start at the beginning of the funnel and work my way down trying to identify where the misleading data might be creeping into the process. In terms of conversion funnels, it is always important to consider the source of the traffic coming into your funnel in the first place. If your marketing team creates a compelling campaign, they might drive a ton of traffic to your landing page. That creates a huge number at the top of your funnel. If that traffic isn't well qualified (maybe the visitors don't meet the requirement for disposable income to be able to afford your product), they will "bounce" off your landing page once they see the price without doing anything else. That will create a high "bounce rate" and will also drive your conversion numbers down. Five purchases out of 100 visits is 5%. Five purchases out of 500 visits is 1%. The same user experience can deliver both those conversion rates depending on how well qualified the traffic coming into the site is, so it's good to understand that before digging into the rest.

In our original ecommerce example, the issue wasn't that our conversion rate was too low, though. The concern there was that it might be artificially high. What might cause that? Our conversion number is made by dividing the number of visits that ended on the checkout confirmation page (5) by the number of visits (100) = 5%. What if the number at the bottom of the funnel is wrong? How could that even be the case? It's a count of the successful orders, so it should be easy to match up with the actual transactions that deposit money into the company account. In this case, what we discovered is that the actual number of transactions that deposited money in the account was three instead of five. Where did those other two orders come from, and where did the money go if not into the company account?

Now would be a good time to create a more narrowly focused report that only includes data from those visits with a confirmation page view. By doing this, your report should only show those five visits. With that report created, you can see that three of your orders came from individuals in different parts of the country. Two of your orders came from the same location. This isn't necessarily odd. What is odd, though, is that both orders happened at exactly the same time of day on different days and both orders included the exact same items. Seeing this type of thing would lead me to believe I might be looking at a bot vs. an actual human. The most likely culprit, in this case, would be something our internal team has set up to verify that the system is up and running exactly as expected. A quick check-in with someone on the Quality Assurance (QA) team verifies that a system is set up to run test orders on the production site using test credit cards that trigger the system to show the confirmation page without actually processing the order.

With that information, the mystery is solved, and the conversion rate of 3% looks a lot more in line with expectations. Knowing that, I would feel more confident moving onto the rest of the process of refining the system. Please keep in mind that it's just as likely that this story could end with either validation that your team had achieved a sustainable 5% conversion rate or that the mystery might not have been solved, and so it would have to be something you keep on your radar as you continue to work on improving the system.

Most importantly, what I want you to take away from this is that it is healthy to apply critical thinking skills, remain curious, and always try to validate your numbers so that that information you rely on isn't misleading you.

Google Analytics

Advancements in usage analytics have been astounding at each step since I began using WebTrends around 2003. Since then, a lot of players have entered the scene with varying levels of success. These days it seems like everyone is using Google Analytics at some level. That doesn't mean they don't have other tools as well, but I can't think of a company I've worked for within the last decade that didn't at least have Google Analytics set up to capture their basic usage information. Many critics will say that Google Analytics is overly complex and offers too many options. I find it to be very easy to install and begin gathering information, so if you don't have anything else, that's where I suggest you start. It is free, and if you need help a lot of consultants are available who can help you configure it to capture and highlight the data and information that is most important for your business.

One important note to keep in mind about Google Analytics and other analytics packages that rely on JavaScript to capture your system usage is that they won't capture complete failure events like 500 (system) errors. This is important, because it doesn't matter how great your user experience is if users aren't seeing it due to the system malfunctioning. I'm sure you would like to think that your engineering teams will be on top of this, but my experience shows that it doesn't hurt to have a set of eyes from the product team checking in on system performance. Check in with your dev/engineering team to see what they are using to monitor system health and ask to have access to the reports. Those system health reports should be looking at the server log files, and those will include failure events as well as the standard usage information.

Mouseflow

I've been using Mouseflow for a very long time to help my customers understand what users are actually doing while using their systems. Unlike other analytics tools that simply show you usage data in charts and tables, Mouseflow creates a video recording of the user session so you can watch exactly what the users did. This kind of visibility is simply astounding and provides insights that are impossible to get from any other tool I've used. Showing a CEO a chart that says users aren't converting well doesn't tell the CEO very much other than your system isn't working well. Showing that same CEO a video of users failing to check out because they couldn't figure out how to enter their gift card information, and then explaining that you believe this issue is causing the drop in conversions represented in a chart, is a lot more compelling.

Instead of standing before your team powerlessly explaining that conversions are down, you can stand before them with that same information along with a potential cause so that they can move forward and address that problem. If you are not 100% certain that the gift card issue was causing all of the conversion issues, you can continue to watch user sessions and try to identify other issues while your team is implementing a fix for the issue you already identified.

The value of Mouseflow for startups cannot be overstated. Startups more than anyone need to understand how their initial customers are using their offering. If there are problems, identifying them quickly can make the difference between a blogger posting something great or focusing on a negative issue that he or she encountered while testing the service. These early formative days in a startup have a lasting impact on the trajectory and eventual success or failure, so maximizing every user interaction is essential.

A great example of that just happened at a startup I'm working with. We launched our first iteration for a quick check with close friends. The goal was to make sure the system was working as expected before we opened usage up to a group of about 70 users we had been talking to that represented our key demographic.

During the first round of testing, we only invited a handful of very close acquaintances. One of those participants made us aware that he encountered a bug that prevented him from being able to access one of our key features. We were surprised by that because none of us in the company had run into that issue yet. We also tried to duplicate the problem, but were unable to.

I can tell you with 100% certainty that if we didn't have Mouseflow, this issue would have fallen between the cracks. I've seen it countless times. An issue occurs and either the product team never hears about it or it gets mentioned by a very small number of users even though it is happening to many of them. Once the product team is made aware of the issue, they try to duplicate it but are unable to. Many times this is where the follow-up will die on the vine.

In some cases, a member of the product team will reach out to someone on the development or QA teams and see if they can duplicate the reported issue or if they might know what could be causing it to happen. In many cases, this is the next place follow-up will die on the vine. One of the team members will create a bug ticket without the ability to demonstrate how to duplicate the issue, and that bug ticket will sit in limbo until the issue gets reported again with a high enough volume that it finally becomes a priority to fix.

This type of issue simply doesn't show up using a tool like Google Analytics or something similar. It's possible that after having thousands of users your team might notice that a key feature is getting less usage than they expected, but without follow-up user interviews or enough specific bug reports the team could just as reasonably assume that users were not interested in that feature as opposed to it being an issue with the system.

My guess is that without Mouseflow, this issue—which we discovered while testing with our first five users—would have continued to impact users for months before anything was done about it. It's not unreasonable for me to say that it might have taken even longer, and all the while negatively impacting user success and perception.

Since we did have Mouseflow installed I was able to observe the issue happening to another user two days after it was first reported. I let the development team know and they watched the recording. We couldn't tell what was causing the problem from the video, but the video confirmed that the issue reported earlier wasn't a one-time thing and gave us a place to begin the process of troubleshooting. Another great feature Mouseflow has is the ability to pipe information from the user session into the reporting in the form of tags. In this case, the recording we had of the user that illustrated the problem also had a session ID tagged in Mouseflow. By combining the issue with a specific session, the dev team was able to go right to the specific log entries for this session to see what the problem was. Although we weren't able to figure out exactly what was wrong at that moment, we had a lot more information and we knew with confidence that it was a real issue that needed to be solved.

A few days later the dev team was able to track down the specific issue and create a fix. Understanding that issue made us aware that we needed better backend tracking in place and also showed us that we had a number of other issues that needed to be fixed. Having tools like Mouseflow to help you detect and resolve issues that could have otherwise gone unnoticed or unresolved can literally be the difference between the success or failure of your entire effort.

Reverse Path Analysis to Understand Failure

It is easy to imagine how looking at a conversion funnel can help you understand how many of your users are succeeding at completing a specific end goal. What might not be so obvious is how you can also use your analytics to create reverse paths from key

This sort of thing happens all the time, and many top designers and developers will state that they don't want to work for large companies because of the general feeling that most lose their ability to innovate once they reach a certain size.

It is important to continue to ask questions and push your team to understand real customer needs while innovating at every stage of your business, or risk being overtaken by a competitor that is. That means respectfully questioning the status quo and using data to explore and identify opportunities that have yet to be uncovered. BlackBerry sat comfortably on the top of its market while Apple was developing the iPhone. Many reading this might not even know what a BlackBerry is, but I bet everyone reading this knows what an iPhone is.

Even small companies can run into problems with fear of change. I once worked for an online retailer where the marketing and merchandising teams wouldn't let anyone change the products on the home page because those products were the best sellers. In this case, the question you need to ask is what if those items are the best sellers because they are on the home page? The results you are seeing could be a self-fulfilling prophecy.

What if we swapped those products out for others that have a higher profit margin? What if we swapped the home page products with others that create a higher average order value? Your team needs to think critically about the decisions that are being made, have ways to communicate their concerns respectfully, and they need ways to test their hypothesis when a new approach seems promising.

Ease the Fear of Change with A/B Testing

A/B testing is a great way to get real-world data about how an alternative approach will perform within your market. Many other methods could be used, but none will provide as clear an understanding as A/B testing will because you will be testing your hypothesis directly with your target audience in direct competition with another hypothesis you have. All the focus groups in the history of the world won't give you as much real-world actionable information as running a well-designed A/B test.

Google Analytics Optimize and Optimizely are good options, but the specific tool isn't what is important. Testing exactly one idea against exactly one variation will help eliminate any question about what impacted the results and help you focus on changes that are identified as the winners. Being able to keep your old approach as one of the options will help alleviate the fear of change, while allowing enough flexibility for your team to feel comfortable running an iterative process of constant innovation. With new data showing better performance against KPIs, it is much easier to have conversations with the leadership team about the changes you are proposing. If instead the numbers show that the old way is still the best way, that's great for the team to understand as well.

There is no need to fix what isn't broken, but your team needs to be able to evaluate their options regularly without fear to help ensure you are being as successful as possible.

Lastly, you need to be aware that sometimes your tests won't really be conclusive. This was one of the most startling things to me because I always assumed one approach would be noticeably better than another. This is often not the case. You'll change the main call to action. No impact. You'll feature all new products on the home page and see only slight shifts in your numbers. This can be frustrating, but it is all part of the game. There will also be times when you change one word on a button and see a huge lift on a primary conversion rate. You have to take the good with the bad as well as the inconclusive and keep on trying in the face of it all.

Some Helpful Tools of the Trade

Back in Chapter 1 I introduced Google's HEART framework for tracking your user experience using a robust and repeatable process. As I have mentioned previously, establishing a well-defined process for tracking progress is essential to the success of the entire iterative improvement process. To help you as you begin to establish your approach to measuring the impact if your efforts I've included more detailed information on how you can start collecting and reviewing the data.

H = Happiness

To collect this type of information you'll need to hear directly from the user. You can get this kind of feedback in person (tradeshows, etc.) or online (social media/reviews). You can also use tools like Feedbackify or Drift to allow your users to reach out directly with their thoughts.

> Feedbackify—Allows users to provide feedback and Net Promoter Scoring (NPS)
> Drift—Inline chat functionality for your service

E = Engagement

This is a measure of how often users are interacting with your service or brand. Google Analytics *repeat visitors* is one way to get this data. If you have it configured properly, you'll be able to track user sessions to pinpoint engagement by user type.

A = Adoption

Adoption is a measure of how many new users you are acquiring. The number of new users / total number of users should be something you can get from your dev team if you aren't capturing it anywhere else.

R = Retention

This is a measure of the % of users are you keeping vs. losing on a month-to-month basis. You should be able to measure the number of registered users you have at the beginning of a specific time frame. Then all you need to do is measure that same discuss what happened with the teams most closely related to the work so they have the insight and understanding required to move on to the next step of dealing with whatever issues your last round of changes exposed. Finally, you'll need to be able to present the findings to your leadership team in a way that honestly communicates the results and frames them in terms of the opportunity the next iteration represents. While I don't strictly believe the old saying that "one shouldn't bring problems to their boss unless they also have a proposed solution," I do recommend having a complete story to tell the leadership team, and that story should include your recommendations whenever possible.

Although there is more political drama involved when things don't go well, the process of planning your next iteration doesn't change much based on the results of the previous round. In general, you'll need to complete the following steps to understand what happened based on your previous changes and move forward strategically.

Research

First, you need to do the research to document the impact of the changes your team made. Hopefully, you planned for this in advance and have a system in place for what you'll measure to be able to gauge your success. In most cases, you'll be looking at a specific Key Performance Indicator (KPI), such as the average order value (AOV) for a product or service. In other cases, you'll be more focused on task success. For example, when I was working for UpToDate we were very concerned with reducing the number of clicks it took doctors to find answers to the questions that arose in their everyday clinical practice. In that case, a key KPI was "clicks to complete" or "time on task."

Sometimes you can't get your results by looking solely at analytics. Sometimes you'll need to moderate a test session with participants to understand the impact of your changes. Whatever method you use, the most important thing to do is ensure that the data you collect is complete and accurate. If you have any questions about the completeness or accuracy of your data, make sure to note that so the team can keep that in mind during analysis.

Finally, don't get tunnel vision. You'll need to continue to keep an eye on the overall health of the system as you explore the impact of your changes. It isn't always obvious that your changes might negatively impact some other part of the system while showing positive results on the KPI you were focusing on. If you keep an eye on the overall health of the system, it will be easier for you to catch unexpected outcomes in what you thought were unrelated areas. If your team is looking at average order value and they see a large rise, that might be considered great. At the same time, if the AOV increase was directly related to the sale of products that require a lot more manual customization, this change might be negatively impacting operational efficiency and therefore represent a net decrease in overall profitability. This is an example of why having something like the HEART framework set up is so important in helping to provide broader insight into the overall health of the system.

Analysis

Lack of analysis is where I see most companies fail at their iterations. This is one of the saddest realities of working in the software industry right now. Teams talk about Agile, Lean UX, iterative development, user-centered design, and UX all day, every day only to have the usage data go ignored or misunderstood because the team doesn't have the required skills to do the analysis and make recommendations.

One company I worked at had all those key pieces in place, including a world-class research team. When I joined the company I was stunned to learn that the research summaries would get sent around and most people on the teams would quickly glance at them and then file them away, never to look at them again. I thought this was simply madness, so I started to review the research and begin the time-intensive process of doing the analysis to identify opportunities and make specific recommendations.

This critical step is the only way the research information gets transformed into potential business outcomes. Without this step, the best the researchers could hope for is that something in their summaries would be so powerfully glaring that a product owner would notice it and create a user story from it rather than just filing it in an archive.

Needless to say, the process of reviewing all the research that had previously been ignored was taking me a while, and when a member of the executive team found out that's what I was doing I was immediately retasked with some very tactical work on a pet project of his. This is where the entire process goes to die. If the team isn't given the time and resources needed to analyze the data, don't even bother with the rest of the process. It is all a huge waste of time and money if your team isn't going to use the output intelligently.

You don't have to fall into that trap. The best way I know to ensure that your team maximizes the value of the data is to keep everyone involved at some level. Some ways to do that include:

- The UX team, developers, and QA should validate that your data collection is working properly so that the data is clean. The product team should be involved as well. Any issues should be brought to the wider team and discussed.
- The research team should present the summary data regularly and encourage questions. I say "summary" here because people get lost in the details and there

is a fair amount of noise, so anything the research team can do to summarize the information will help people stay engaged and keep the conversations focused. Having a shared resource where all the detailed research can be accessed will provide those with interest all the data the team has collected.

- The UX team should present its findings and recommendations regularly and encourage questions. This part of the process is very engaging because it brings the work full circle. I've heard many times from many different teams that they wonder what the results of project x, y, or z was. Often they'll nervously laugh because they know that not knowing the results means the process has fallen apart somewhere.

- If the UX team can present the results, findings, and recommendations, it not only tells the team what happened, but also what the team might be able to do next. There is a lot to be said about the impact this has on morale within a company. Working hard into the night is a lot easier if you know that the results of that work will be tracked, and hopefully the team will be celebrating a success in the near future.

- The product team should celebrate the wins and discuss the losses openly and honestly with an eye toward what can be learned. This is the final step in bringing the work full circle. Often the product team is indirectly leading the direction of the efforts of many teams, including design, research, development, and QA.

Hearing, in a public way, about how a team effort created a great business outcome says a lot about the value of each member of the team and is a great way to share recognition for a job well done. When the results are not great, it is still helpful to share and discuss as a team so that everyone can be a part of the solution.

Findings

Research teams vary widely in terms of their ability to do the analysis and summarize findings. As a rule, more specialized research teams produce better data, but usually do not provide analysis and recommendations. On the other hand, teams that don't have formal research departments and rely more on their UX team end up with data that isn't quite as good, but oftentimes have great analysis and recommendation capabilities. These are generalizations based on what I've seen and are in no way meant to put your team in a box.

If your team is different, do your best to look for the strengths and weaknesses and bolster wherever you see shortcomings. Ideally, your team would have both and get the best of both worlds. With that said, in many cases you will be the only person on the team who is doing the research and analysis and making the recommendations. In this scenario, you'll want to get others involved to check your work early and often to help ensure that your team is making the best decisions possible, and because buy-in comes from cooperation, openness, and communication.

Whatever the makeup of your team, you'll need to follow the same basic approach to documenting and communicating your findings:

1 Complete a detailed review of the data and document the individual findings at a high level. I usually capture the data in a spreadsheet so I can keep track of everything and spot recurring issues or themes. A recurring issue is an issue that happens with more than one testing participant, and a recurring theme is when multiple participants encounter similar, but not identical, issues. An example might be that one participant was unable to update her profile because she didn't know that the word "Profile" was clickable due to lack of affordance. Another participant was unable to navigate to the system preferences because he didn't know the word "Preferences" was clickable. Both of these issues share a common theme of poor affordance, but they are not the same exact issue.

2 Review all the data to look for patterns. This can be as simple as keeping track of how many participants encountered specific issues. This is one place confirmation bias can slip in. If you went into this study thinking the outcomes might include something specific, and early on in the results you see some data to support that conclusion, it is easy to conclude that you were right.

To protect against bias impacting your reporting, I recommend quantifying issues in terms of:

1. Occurrence (number of participants who encountered this issue)

2. Severity (did it simply interrupt the participants' progress or completely block their progress?)

3. Frequency (will this issue always happen during task completion or is it avoidable once participants are aware of it?)

Doing this helps your team understand issues in ways that will help with prioritization, and it helps keep you and the other reviewers honest and unbiased.

3 If you spot patterns, go back and look for ways to prove or disprove those patterns. In general, you need to think like a skeptic here and make sure you can answer the obvious questions someone might ask to prove or disprove what you are reporting. Luck favors the well-prepared, and taking some time for this step will help avoid embarrassing moments in meetings.

4 Create an item-by-item review of each key finding in detail. This is usually where I'm creating the individual slides for each issue that I'll use in my final report. Sometimes they are slides; sometimes they are pages in a PDF. Either way, this is where I'm telling the story of this specific issue. These pages/slides usually end up being the bulk of the presentation.

To document each issue, I usually follow a very similar format as seen in Figure 6.1 that includes:

1. The task description where the issue occurred.

2. A description of the issue itself.

3. A chart that shows how many participants encountered this issue.

4. An annotated screenshot that illustrates the issue.

5. Any supporting participant quotes I can find in the results. This is usually the most impactful piece of information I can provide. In best-case scenarios, I've captured the participant encountering the issue on video. In that case, if I'm presenting slides I'll also include the video. Nothing helps members of your team understand an issue and the impact it is having on users like a video.

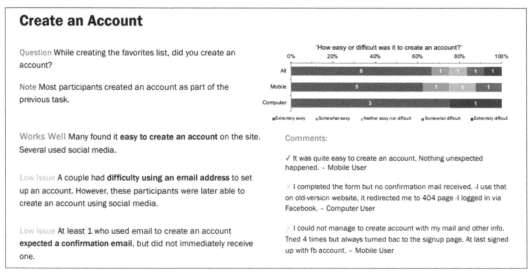

Figure 6.1: An illustration of a completed finding slide

This is what many of my finding slides look like. I don't always follow the same format and I encourage you to explore what works best for you, but this approach works often so it's my fallback.

Recommendations

If you observed that your users were clicking the sign-up button on your landing page but then noticed that only a small number of users actually completed the sign-up process, there are some baseline assumptions you could make.

My first thought would be that there might be a technical issue that is causing users to fail their sign-up. This would be my first assumption because the sign-up process isn't something extraordinary or new. Most sign-up processes are essentially the same, and if the one I'm researching doesn't deviate from that standard much, my assumption is that the backend system is failing in some way.

My second thought would be that there is something the team overlooked in our design of the sign-up flow that is causing confusion.

Lastly, I would start to wonder if there is something about the service itself that users are backing away from once they are in the sign-up process.

Don't get hung up on the order of those potential issues. The important takeaway is that the quantitative data (the what) shows there is an issue, and at the moment we'll assume I don't have any qualitative data (the why) to review to figure out exactly what is happening. Since I don't know what is going on, I take my first couple thoughts on what it could be and begin the process of researching what it might be. In this situation I may eventually recommend that the team spend the time and money to do a qualitative study to narrow it down, but for now my approach would be to see if there is anything obvious that matches my initial concerns.

To kick off my research in this case, I would send an email out to the QA or dev team to see if they are already aware of any system errors involving the sign-up process. If they aren't aware of any, I would ask them to check the time range in question and see if they can verify that all was running as expected. This might take the dev team some time, so from there I would move on to researching my next thought.

To review the system for issues, I would essentially conduct a heuristic eval on the sign-up process and walk through all the required steps myself to see if there is something I missed while designing it in the first place. Simultaneously I would be considering my third concern that related to users backing out of the sign-up process because of something they learned about the service.

My last-ditch effort before considering a qualitative study would be to contact the company support team and check in with them on how often they get support calls related to the sign-up process to see if they can offer any insights.

It is entirely possible that the actual issue is something you may never have thought of, but what's important for you to take away from all this is that usually the best person to work on the recommendations will be a UX person because the first step in being able to make a recommendation is to accurately diagnose the problem. Since members of the UX team are usually closest to the design process that created the system, as well as most likely to understand the user groups that are impacted, I believe they have the best chance at diagnosing issues. This is a team sport, so checking in with the rest of the team is always helpful, but my opinion is that UX should lead that effort.

Once you are reasonably sure you understand the issue, you can move on to considering what your recommended solutions might be. In the case of the sign-up example, what I came to conclude was that users became concerned about signing up for the service once they were in the process because we asked for access to files that some users might consider sensitive. They might not have expected that, and we didn't do a good job of helping them understand what to expect before they signed up.

My recommendation in this case was to create a demo that included the entire setup process so that users knew what to expect. This also gave our team an opportunity to directly communicate with users the reason we needed access to their files, that we wouldn't have write access to those files, and what benefit they could expect to get in return.

Without digging into the root cause of the issues that are observed in the research, there is no way to strategically plan to resolve those issues. As I mentioned earlier, lack of root-cause understanding is where I see many teams fail to derive value for their research. Many times, the solutions to problems are relatively trivial once the actual problem is understood. Figure 6.2 shows an example of how to organize recommendations to share with your team.

Prioritization

While documenting the findings you should have started the prioritization process by itemizing the occurrence, severity, and frequency of each finding. That's the first part of the process, and if you were to state what this means to a member of your team, you would say something like "This issue occurred in 6 of 10 sessions (occurrence). Participants who encountered this issue were able to complete their task but spent an average of 3 minutes longer completing the task (severity). Participants understood what the issue was and will be able to avoid it in the future (frequency)."

In summary, if we look at this example issue without considering how it impacts specific personas, I would say it is a mid-level priority issue. It is impacting more than half of the participants, causing users to be less efficient than those who didn't encounter the issue. If this issue were a blocker, meaning that it prevented users from completing their task, it would have been considered a high-priority item, but since participants were not likely to have to deal with the issue in the future, it is a mid-level issue.

That's only half the story, though, because we still need to consider what personas this issue impacts.

If we have a mid-level issue that affects our highest-priority personas, then the issue will likely be considered high priority. This is where understanding, documenting, and communicating the relative priority of your personas is very important. Just like setting your goals, strategies, and objectives is very important in helping your team make decisions, having clearly prioritized personas will help your team take this next step to be able to make the important decisions necessary to schedule the most important work first.

Usability Evaluation
Checkout - 02/15/2020

Kevin Braun

Section	Issue Description	Example	Potential Resolutions	Impact	Difficulty	How to A/B
Cart	Users do not read large blocks of copy unless that copy represents the content they were looking for in the first place. Instead users scan the page looking for important information. The bulk of the "create an account" information in the checkout is currently in one large run-on sentence. "When you create an account, you can receive free standard shipping for orders $45 and up, earn rewards points for every beverage you purchase, work towards Platinum Member discount pricing, log on to check your order status and more. It's a winning combination. Get started today!"	Screen	Individually call out the value propositions to promote comprehension and scannability. **Create a free account to:** -Receive free standard shipping for orders **$45 and up** -Earn rewards points for every beverage you purchase -Work towards Platinum Member discount pricing -Log on to check your order status and more. **It's a winning combination. Get started today!**	High	Low	Create a B version that breaks out the individual value propositions and test. Other versions could also be created using color, size and, font to emphasize the value.
Cart / Checkout	Showing totals that include discounts but not the starting price is confusing.	Screen	Show largest total number at the top, then show discounts, then shipping and taxes, and then a well-defined total.	High	Low / Medium	Create a B version that includes the starting price and details the discounts etc. and test
Checkout	Text fails section 508 accessibility guidelines for readability.	Screen	Increase text size and color contrast to improve readability and visual hierarchy.	High	Low	Create a B version with improved size. Create a C version with improved contrast. Create a D version with both improved and test.

Figure 6.2: A spreadsheet or slide like this that shows issues as well as their priority and recommendations will help communicate your findings to your team.

If you are working for a startup, all of your initial users might have the same priority. If you are working at a small, established company, the priority of your users might be in flux from quarter to quarter depending on the goals of the company. It is entirely possible that the board of directors might tell your leadership team to focus on acquisition, and that shift in focus might change the prioritization. The entire team needs to be made aware of any changes so that everyone stays on the same page. Few things are more frustrating than finding out the work you have been doing was deprioritized a month ago and no one told your team.

I'm not very dogmatic about a specific approach to this other than to say that I consider the issue priority as well as how that issue impacts the highest-priority users to determine the overall priority. Usually this process is straightforward, but it is good to validate that the team agrees with the overall priority and resolve any differences as they occur.

Effort

Effort is the wildcard in the process. The clearest example of that I can give is time travel. If I ask 100 people, it is safe to say that most would like a time machine if I could give it to them. If I look at the people who can pay me the most for it, that group is likely to show very strong interest. That being the case, I would have a feature that is very much desired in the market and those potential customers with the most resources would be glad to pay me for it. At face value, that would be a very high-priority item. The effort required to make it happen is what kills the deal. This is why it is so important that your product team takes effort into account before scheduling the work.

With your candidates for the next iteration prioritized in your backlog based on the issue itself and the personas that are impacted, it is a good time to reach out to your design and development teams to have them help the rest of the team understand the effort required. To do that they'll need to provide a SWAG (Scientific Wild Ass Guess) for each candidate item in the backlog. Once you have your priorities and your SWAGs, your team can move forward with confidence to schedule the most valuable and viable work for your next iteration.

As the teams dig in and start working, it is not out of the question that they might uncover something that changes the effort estimate because SWAGs by their very nature are somewhat of a guess. If that happens, your team will need to meet and discuss options for how to deal with it. In general, the options include leaving everything the same and continue working as planned, changing the scheduling of the item in question and replacing it with the next item in the backlog, or putting a stop on all work related to that issue because it is no longer something that the team can resolve at this time.

If your team decides to stop work and swap in another item from the backlog, make sure to note what happened and why so that what the team learned in this last round won't be lost when it comes time to reconsider the work you shelved.

Further Reading

Depending on your project management style, iteration planning might vary from what I've described. The SAFe (Scaled Agile) folks have a solid article on the topic if you are interested in seeing how others do it:

"Scaled Agile Iteration Plannings"
> www.scaledagileframework.com/iteration-planning

MAKE THESE METHODS WORK FOR YOU

"Measure twice, code once."

—Kevin C. Braun

Starting with a Greenfield Project or at a Startup

Congratulations. You are kicking things off and you need to begin the process of taking a rough idea and turning it into a polished product. The first step is to document exactly what the current plan is so everyone on the team has the same understanding:

1. What is the idea?
2. Who does it solve a problem for?
3. What problem does it solve for those people?
4. How is it better at solving this problem than its competitors?
5. How will this idea be monetized?

With this information, the team can begin to verify that the original idea is on the right track and identify places where adjustments need to be made. To do that you'll need to dig deep into the market to understand what it currently wants, how much it is willing to pay, and how competitors are currently delivering on what is needed.

Understanding the Market

You can think of the market almost as a macro-persona. Some businesses will target multiple markets while others focus on one market exclusively. Either way, you need to understand and define at least one market as part of your process for evaluating and refining your business and your product(s). The process for researching the market isn't all that different from researching individual persona needs. At this early stage, your recruiting efforts will be broader than later in the process when you have more data to create specific personas.

Identifying Market Representatives

If you have investors, they should be able to put you in touch with some solid market research participants. Even with that advantage, you'll likely need to reach out to your team's network and get more participants. Honestly, at this stage the more you can get, the better. Ideally, you'll have somewhere between 25 and 100 well-qualified market representatives that represent the various user groups you intend to solve problems for. If you are struggling to find participants and they represent an easy-to-find demographic, usertesting.com is a great and inexpensive place to start. If you have a hard-to-find or very specific demographic, Applause (www.applause.com) is ideal because they can find users in the most challenging cases.

If this process feels daunting, it should. Recruiting for your research is going to be a challenge and it is one that you'll want to get a head start on. Targeting 50 or so participants in your first three months should provide your team with a good foundation of market information to build on.

One final thought on this: I don't always do this step. I'm currently working on developing a product with a friend. We are entirely bootstrapping this idea, and our approach is to build something MVP-ish as soon as possible to test with users. We'll essentially do all the market work after doing the first round of design so that we can show the user something specific as we have our discussions. When I'm working on larger projects or a project that has any level of funding, I like to do the work to dig deep into the market first.

Writing an Interview Script

As you work to recruit, you'll want to draft an interview script. I can't overstate the importance of the script. It might be tempting to consider having free-form conversations with your participants that cover the key concepts. I can tell you from firsthand experience that this makes the analysis process very painful, and your results will invariably be incomplete because free-form conversations have a way of straying off-topic. Trust me on this and create a script that you stick to for your interviews. When you have done your

Table 7.1 Sample Interview Agenda

Section	Time Allotment
Intros	5:00 minutes
Highest-priority tasks	15:00 minutes
Tools they use	10:00 minutes
Highest-priority issues	10:00 minutes
Your solution pitch	10:00 minutes
Their perception of your pitch	10:00 minutes

analysis and have a compelling story to tell that is backed up with data, it will be worth the effort.

If I've convinced you to write a script, I recommend keeping your sessions to 60 minutes, so depending on what you need to cover it might make sense to break up your script into the sections outlined in Table 7.1.

Obviously I don't know what you are building so these are general buckets. Adjust as needed. If you have well-qualified candidates you should be able to get useful information in these time frames. Make sure the participants are aware of these time restrictions in your intro so they understand what to expect. Keep an eye on the clock so that you can step in and keep the conversation on track. You can always ask the really interesting participants if they can spend more time with you or schedule a follow-up session.

When writing your script you might find it helpful to narrow the questions to focus the responses on the most valuable information. An example would be to ask "What are the three most common tasks you perform?" vs. asking "What are the most common tasks you perform?" That more open-ended question might take longer to answer, and without the "most common" qualifier you might not get to the most important information if you must cut them off due to time.

Make sure not to write leading questions. As I mentioned in Chapter 5, a classic example of a leading question is "Washington, great president or greatest president?" This question leaves no possibility of saying anything negative about George Washington. If you reported the results of this question, the worst it could possibly be is 10 out of 10 participants stated that George Washington was a great president. Some unscrupulous people who participate in the Fake UX (FaUX) process I mentioned previously will do this intentionally, but it is easy to accidentally write questions that are biased in some way, so pay attention to your questions and make sure you are encouraging open and honest responses. Sometimes the truth will hurt, but whatever that truth is will eventually come to light, and it is a lot less painful when you learn about it early in the process rather than when your team has spent months or years building something no one wants.

Another reason to make sure you have done your prep work is that participants disengage in sessions they feel aren't really relevant to them. I saw this firsthand in a recent study that I wasn't running but was invited to. When many of the questions don't directly apply to the participants, they are going to feel like the session is a waste of time and you likely will as well. In general, if your participants are screened well and your questionnaire is focused on them, they'll likely provide useful feedback.

Let uncomfortable pauses happen when listening to responses. If you ask a question and the participant pauses, the moderator will often step in and add some clarification or otherwise try to prompt the participant. I encourage you not to do that because many times the participants are simply forming their thoughts. They may end up asking you a clarifying question that you hadn't considered. That would be a great finding, and interrupting them may prevent that from happening. The time it takes them to respond can be a finding in itself. If you ask someone what they think of your pitch and they immediately and enthusiastically say they love it and then follow that up by articulating the key points that they enjoyed, you can feel pretty confident that they meant it. If, on the other hand, they pause and think and then end up just saying "Yeah, I like it . . . it's good" but can't really articulate why, then that's an indicator that they are being polite but are not really on board with your pitch.

Sometimes when I sense that the response wasn't the full truth, I'll ask a follow-up stating something like "It seemed like you were hesitant in your response. Do you agree there was a hesitation, and if so, what do you think caused it?" Many times participants will laugh a little when you ask the follow-up question, but usually whatever they say next is going to get to the heart of their feelings. Other times they will just say something like "No, I was just trying to make sure I had it clear in my head before answering." Either way, when in doubt ask that follow-up question and you'll feel a lot more confident in the response you report to your team.

The Notes

You should record every session so you can refer back to the recording during analysis and possibly share small portions of the recordings with your team for emphasis. Oftentimes, nothing is more motivating than listening to a well-respected, well-qualified participant provide feedback on your service. This helps take the team's personal opinions and preferences out of the equation and creates confidence in the recommendations.

The recordings and your notes serve as the foundation of your findings. I usually take notes during the session, and I'll revisit those notes right after the session is over to clean them up and call out the key points. I know that not everything I write is going to be noteworthy, and dealing with that by cleaning up my notes right when the session ends helps separate the signal from the noise. If I wait too long to do this, I won't remember all of the context and I'll end up having to take the notes at face value.

If I am having a particularly good day, I'll manage to capture some time stamps during the conversation to go along with my notes. Anything I can do to make the analysis phase of the project easier will improve the results. Zoom Video Conferencing has some great tools built-in, and one is the ability to transcribe your recordings. This is incredibly helpful, but note-taking is still important to help surface the key things you observed.

Iterating on Your Script

During your interviews you will likely want to make changes to your script based on what you are hearing in the sessions. There are two kinds of changes. One is an immediate need, and the other is one you find that might benefit the next study. Changing things in your questionnaire once you have already started your interviews has the potential to negate the value of the previous participants, so it is something you should do only if there is a fundamental problem. An immediate change is only warranted in my mind if you recognize that the question itself is leading or otherwise faulty in a way that will harm the integrity of the study. Hopefully you will catch that sort of thing before talking with participants, but things like this happen so it is good to have a plan.

The less urgent changes are great to keep track of so that when your team is planning the next study you can take that knowledge into the kick-off process. Sometimes the changes that occur to me aren't really representative of a shortcoming in the current study. Sometimes I just happen to realize that something in particular will be great to dig into so I end up noting it. These kinds of items are easy to lose track of, so at least create a shared document and include your thoughts with a date and some context.

The Analysis

If you did your job right in setting up and conducting your interviews, the analysis should be only a little painful. I say that because although I find the results of studies like this exciting, the analysis is the most "heads down" intensive part of the process and it always feels like a chore to me. Maybe you'll love it, but this is the main reason I don't specialize in research. I can do only so many studies in a row before I need to do some hands-on design work so I can feel better.

If you were loose with your process and didn't follow your script, it is going to take a lot longer to tie everything back together into a cohesive report. Either way, your best friend in this process is going to be a tool that takes your recordings and automatically creates a transcription as Zoom does. If you have that you can simply open a specific interview, search for a keyword from the first question in your questionnaire, and jump right to the results. Before this technology was widely available researchers would spend endless hours scrubbing back and forth in video or audio files looking for the start of the next question. Being able to listen to exactly what the participant said while also having the text in front of you to search is incredibly powerful and speeds up the process tremendously.

While doing my analysis, I keep track of how each participant answers in relation to their part of the demographic groupings in the study so that I don't have to go back and tally that at the end. All this means is that I take note of their response so that I have a detailed report of them as a participant, but I also increment a counter for each question in relation to their gender, age range, geographic location, etc. This way, at the end I can say what each individual's responses were as well as how each demographic group responded so the team gets a segmented understanding as well. Having the detailed individual results is helpful as well for a number of reasons, but a key reason is that it allows your team to go back to the data and see if they can get other questions answered that were not part of the original study.

Once you are done with your analysis, you can write up your summary of the results. Finally, you can start the process of creating your recommendations. Sometimes it might just be you writing the recommendations, but if you are on a bigger team you can run a meeting where you all review the results and the summary to brainstorm together to determine the best recommendations.

With all that information collected and organized, you can take the final step of creating a report of your results. You should take this part seriously because this report will communicate the quality of the work you have done. If it appears thrown together, that may discredit your work. If it is polished and professional, people will instinctively expect that the work has been conducted in a professional manner and trust it more. You don't need an amazing design template or anything, but the report should include a title page, overview and methodology, participants, a summary, question-by-question results, and recommendations. See Figures 7.1 through 7.6 for examples. Note that you'll

Figure 7.1: A title page should include the project name, date, the author(s), and sponsor.

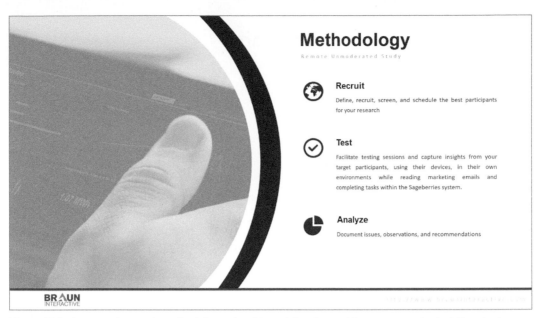

Figure 7.2: An overview and methodology should explain why and how you conducted the study.

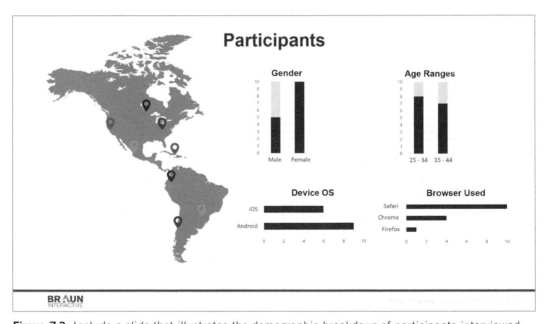

Figure 7.3: Include a slide that illustrates the demographic breakdown of participants interviewed.

want to mention what testing method you used so anyone reading the report will know what type of data is being reviewed.

In the end, make the report your own and make sure it fits the study you are reporting on. However, if you decide to deviate from these suggested guidelines, do so purposefully

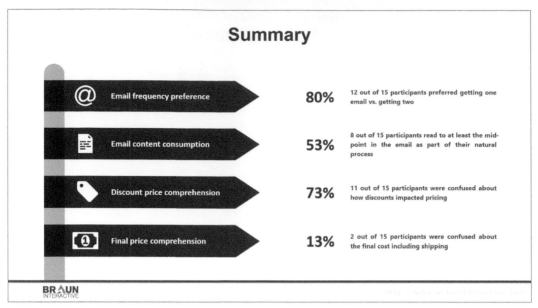

Figure 7.4: A summary presents the high-level results and sets the stage for the detailed slides that follow.

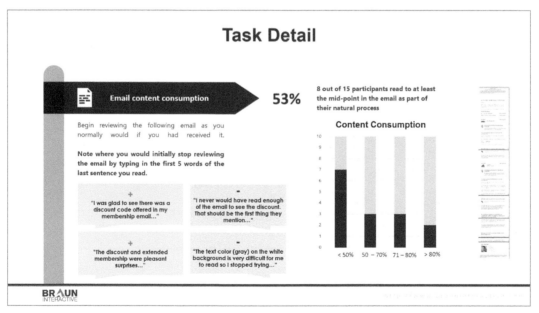

Figure 7.5: Question-by-question results cover the detailed results on a question-by-question basis.

Recommendations

Task	Issue	Example	Recommendation	Impact
Content Consumption	Roughly 50% of participants discovered the discount code.	Screen	Improve discoverability by moving the call to action to the beginning of the content	High
Cart Comprehension	Showing totals that include discounts but not the starting price is confusing	Screen	Show the largest total number at the top, then subtract discounts, then add shipping and taxes	High
Checkout	Text fails section 508 accessibility testing for readability	Screen	Select and test your font size and colors to improve readability	High
Confirmation Page	The 2nd line of the address is not shown, causing users to call support	Screen	Include all address information on the confirmation page so users can verify their order.	High

BRAUN INTERACTIVE

Figure 7.6: Include a slide to present your prioritized recommendations.

so that if someone asks you why you didn't include a specific part, you'll have a good answer.

The Market Review

As part of the process of documenting your company's current understanding of your market, you'll want to identify three to five competitors or companies that offer similar services in other industries.

Once you have your target companies identified, you'll want to break each one down by size, market share, offerings, and anything you can document about how they are perceived by the market. You'll want to rank them so that you can identify one as the leader while tracking the others to see if they gain or lose traction as time goes on.

Your competitors may or may not be all that important to you early on. If they are, it's likely that you'll be focused on surpassing feature parity and looking for ways to overcome any barriers to market entry that they have been able to establish. Even if what you are able to document is very little, capture what you can as a starting point to build on as you determine what your initial offering will be.

The Customer Journey

One good way to document the current state of the market is to map the customer journey(s). Depending on your industry, there may be more than one typical journey.

to defining a new strategy using what you learned to help guide you, or you iterate on the strategy you already had. The most important thing is that you don't lose sight and start thinking of a strategy as your goal.

Going back to the previous example, a strategy that might help a company become the number one alternative energy monitoring system would be to capture the United States solar performance monitoring market. Another strategy might be to capture the United States wind energy monitoring market, etc.

It is pretty easy to see how capturing one of these large markets would move the company toward its goal, but these strategies need to be broken down further because they are still too high-level for anyone to be making a product plan from.

Those obvious strategies aren't the only ones that should be considered. This is where it is important to run at least one divergent exercise to get your team to explore the possibilities. It is entirely possible that a less obvious strategy like identifying an emerging technology and trying to capture that entire market while it is small might be a really good approach instead of trying to face the large incumbent in an already established market head to head. If your team can achieve that and get some press it might improve your odds when you do face the big competitors in your space.

The specifics of what I just covered aren't important. What is important is that your team takes the time to do the divergent thinking and then comes back together to converge on the strategies you all believe will have the best chance of achieving the goal.

The Objectives

A well-defined objective needs to be measurable and represent a logical breakdown of the larger strategy. In the case of wanting to become the largest solar monitoring company in the United States, it would make sense to break down this problem and have objectives for becoming the industry leader by sales volume in each of the 50 states. This way it is easy to see how the objectives could lead to the desired goal by moving the strategy forward. It is also easy to see how you'll measure success or failure in that, at the end of the year, your company either will or will not be the sales leader in each state, or at least enough states to claim a win by combined sales volume.

It is also important to note that you can make great progress on a strategy by meeting many of its objectives and decide that this is a valid strategy to employ. Although you might not have perfect success, you are seeing enough success with these numbers to want to continue. In other words, a well-executed and valuable strategy doesn't have to be one that went perfectly. It just needs to be moving your company forward toward the goal at least at pace with other strategies.

Lastly, just because the strategy breaks down nicely into objectives that make sense doesn't mean you shouldn't take the time to prioritize those objectives for the team. For example, it is easy to see that California would have more value for a solar monitoring company than Rhode Island in terms of sales volume. With that in mind, your team would likely focus more effort on California while keeping Rhode Island on their list.

You'll need to go through that exercise for each strategy you have until all of your measurable objectives are prioritized. Once you have that done, in order to support your objective it is time to start defining who the customers are. You'll do that by defining personas. This is where we transition from UX strategy into the more traditional user-centered design process.

The Personas

To begin to transition from the UX strategy phase into the more tactical hands-on work, we'll need to break down each objective. This will help the team understand exactly what needs to be done and who it needs to be done for.

Previously I mentioned that the solar monitoring industry is different when you compare what is needed in California vs. what is needed in Rhode Island. I mentioned it specifically to highlight that one is a much bigger market than the other, and winning in California will put the company much closer to its nationwide goal than winning in Rhode Island. Market size isn't the only difference, though. With that comes a lot of very important usage differences that will change the service that you build. In California, your service might be used to monitor everything from individual household rooftop installations all the way up to the world's largest utility-scale projects. In Rhode Island, the largest project you will encounter isn't even 1% of the production of the largest site in California, so the way you approach the business will need to be different.

Seeing this disparity, I would immediately know I needed to consider how this impacts the other 48 objectives, but my guess would be that the business couldn't possibly address the nuanced differences of all 50 states. Based on that I would first try to roughly regionalize the objectives to reduce the number of variables the team had to keep track of. Your team could spend a lot of time trying to find ways to break the regions, but my recommendation would be to keep moving quickly and revisit all of these decisions when you have more data to iterate with.

After reviewing the key geographic differences between the states it might be reasonable to break up the country into four regions, including the northeast, south east, north west, and southwest. For simplicity's sake, we'll use the Mississippi to divide the country into east and west and we'll use the Mason-Dixon Line to divide the country into north and south. It doesn't break down quite that cleanly, so accommodations would need to be made for states like Nevada and California to put them completely in the southwest,

Primary Motivations

Ryan wants to be able to maintain the sites he works on with the lowest maintenance costs possible while helping the team meet their contractual performance benchmarks and guarantees.

Pain Points

- Ryan's team wasn't part of the installation process so they inherit, and need to deal with, whatever shortcomings were built into the system when it was commissioned.
- Many of the installations he manages are in deserts, meaning the panels need to be cleaned on a fixed schedule to ensure that the system is functioning as expected.
- His current monitoring solution isn't as robust as it needs to be. The solution has been working well on smaller systems, but the scale of his bigger projects has caused issues to have gone unnoticed due to problems with the loggers losing data or otherwise not communicating system status.
- No matter how well mapped out the system is, it is still hard to find specific panels in the field when they are reported to be malfunctioning.

Needs

- Accurate, timely status information
- Accurate routine maintenance schedules for all systems he manages
- Issue reporting and resolution tracking across many installations
- Panel-level project mapping and in-the-field wayfinding

Quote

"I need a system that I can access even in some of the most remote locations in CA and AZ that will keep me posted on what needs routine maintenance, alert me of emergencies, and allow me to dispatch members of my team. I also need to be able to update issue status and escalate anything that my team cannot handle so the site owner/operators can call in backup."

With that persona in mind, it is pretty easy to imagine many types of scenarios that could be applicable. For this example, we'll have a look at one that documents Ryan's need to troubleshoot a performance issue within a large system he maintains in the Mojave Desert.

Scenarios should represent real-world usage for the persona they are associated with. It is important that there is a stated result. That desired result serves as the primary focus of the activities the user should be partaking in. Notice the scenario doesn't say anything about the system in this case. By leaving those details out, the team won't be artificially restricted while brainstorming solutions to the three key elements of this scenario. Each persona will likely have multiple associated scenarios.

The next step is for your team to create a solution for this scenario that allows users like Ryan to be able to

1 Get a better understanding of what has happened.

2 Determine what he might need to do to fix it.

3 Identify where the issues are located on the site so he can navigate the maze of panels to find the exact fault in the system to resolve it.

The Product Roadmap Scaffold

Once you have determined who your key users are and what they need to be able to do, you can begin to combine that with what you learned from your market research to create a scaffold for your product roadmap. At this stage in a startup, it is hard to have a solid roadmap but it is helpful to define the direction you have established so that the team can start to look down the road a bit and to be strategic about their planning.

One of the biggest advantages of documenting the current state of the product plan is that you are more likely to spot operational efficiencies and unnecessary time-sinks. If none of your key scenarios require search functionality to be present in the system, you can skip that even though it would otherwise make perfect sense to include it. That doesn't mean you won't end up how the systems will interact rather than an opinion-based solution, this approach can serve as a good foundation to work from.

The only real disadvantage to this approach is that the design team may be on hold while awaiting the results of the conceptual model unless your team takes this on together.

- **Use case development**

  This can be done by representatives from different groups on the team and then reviewed and refined together. It can also be done by one member and then reviewed by the team. The advantage of creating use cases first is that your team is forced to think of task completion in a stepwise format that includes both the user interactions and the system responses. This can create a very holistic representation of how to solve for the scenario as long as the person (or people) creating the use case has a solid understanding of how the system works or will work. Iterating on a use case in text is a lot faster than iterating on wireframe storyboards, so this is usually a step that is recommended before wireframing.

  Once you have a complete use case, your team can go on to create a wireframe for each step in the use case to effectively storyboard the entire experience.

  One disadvantage to this approach is that sometimes you can get ahead of yourself and specify a solution that doesn't take into consideration a technical limitation of your system. Another issue can be that your use case ends up not including enough detail. This usually becomes evident when working on the wireframes and realizing something isn't specified, which would require the designer to solve that issue.

With all that being said, I would recommend starting with the journey map if there are previously existing experiences that solve for the scenario in question. By doing this your team will be able to visualize and discuss the current state of the art for this experience, and if there is data to illustrate how users are feeling at each step, all the better. This data can be captured during interview sessions or from inline feedback submissions. One goal for the UX team is going to be improving user sentiment throughout the experience.

If you are solving a problem that you haven't seen solved before, I would recommend starting with the conceptual model to illustrate all the various processes and systems that will need to be in place to assist the users as they complete their journey. This understanding will provide the design team with some guardrails to help guide their interaction design process. Figure 7.8 is an example of a quick conceptual model I made to help the team I was working with understand how the entire system worked. Once again, my key point here is you shouldn't spend a lot of time creating beautiful artifacts. The information that gets communicated to the team is where the value comes from.

From there, a divergent wireframing exercise with diverse members of your team will help expose the range of possible solutions while giving everyone a voice in the process.

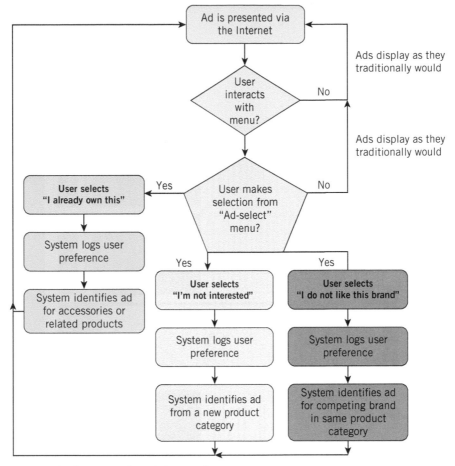

Figure 7.8: Conceptual model example

The team will need to discuss the various approaches and agree on a direction before the session is complete. A quick group wireframing session as shown in Figure 7.9 is a great way to facilitate discussion and ensure that all points of view are considered in your solutions. The "buy-in" created by this type of session is very valuable when a team is working hard to meet deadlines together.

After the direction is identified, the next step would be to write up a detailed step-by-step use case as you'll see in Figure 7.10. Your use cases will serve as a specification of sorts for the design team to create detailed wireframes from. The use case format should be simple, but the value created by documenting each step the user takes and all system responses is very valuable as your team narrows in on a final solution to design and build.

Lastly, the design team should create a complete storyboard that illustrates the agreed-upon experience that solves for the task represented in the scenario as shown in Figure 7.11. This complete storyboard should be reviewed with any changes from the team being made before testing with users that represent the desired demographic. Storyboards should illustrate everything required to solve for the scenario from start to finish, including one wireframe for each step in the use case.

Taxonomy and Information Architecture

Not to be left out of the process are the core taxonomy and information architecture concerns. This part of the process can come at different times depending on the maturity of the system you are working on. I realize many who are dogmatic about the process like to try to do this first and then build the system around the information architecture they have created. For systems that have existed in the market for some time, I don't mind creating a content inventory and mapping that to an information architecture early in the process so that the team has a visual reference of the existing system as we begin the process of improving on it.

For new startups, I think attempts at this that aren't informed by the user-centered design process can drive the experience toward mirroring the underlying structure of the systems that the service is built on. I see this all the time in organically grown services that were initially built by developers with no input from users or designers.

The best example I can give to illustrate why this is a problem is a grocery store. If there were a database of items in the grocery store, it might be completely logical for those items to be stored alphabetically. If the experience for the grocery store was designed based on the structure of that database, all of the items in the store would be organized in the aisles alphabetically as well. That would mean that a customer who wanted to compare the prices between Honeycrisp apples and Red Delicious apples would need to walk many aisles over just to do so. Where this process really breaks down is when the customer walks all that way to find the Red Delicious apples where they should be—in this case, between the rat poison and red velvet cupcakes—only to discover that the store doesn't sell them.

Obviously this isn't the best experience for the user or for the people running the store. It's just as obvious that this approach isn't great for software design, but it has been happening since people first started developing software. It is such a well-understood problem that in the late 1990s Alan Cooper wrote a great book about this called *The Inmates Are Running the Asylum*. Even with this knowledge, it is still a widespread problem in the software industry.

This is why, when working with startups, I like to get a strong understanding of who the users are, what they need to do, and also how our team proposes to design a solution to solve for all that before attempting to go back in and refine the taxonomy and information architecture. Once we have all that information, we are in a good position to leverage our knowledge of the users' mental model as well as the terms they use to describe the elements of their tasks to create an information architecture that is tailored to the expectations of the target users.

Testing

With your wireframes complete, it is time to get some user feedback to understand the real-world impact your work has made before you invest the time required to build it. If you are working with a recruiting/testing company like Applause, this process might be as simple as giving their team access to your work so that they can test it with the participants they have recruited for you. If not, then you'll need to have recruited at least 10 participants that match your demographic and moderate the testing sessions. As I mentioned previously, usertesting.com is a good resource for participants if you are managing the process of recruiting. Your last resort will be identifying connections from within your team network.

Whatever method you end up using to recruit your participants, you'll need to follow the same basic approach you used earlier for the market research. There are a few differences when testing your solution with users, including:

- Your testing sessions will likely take at least an hour. You still need to keep things as short as possible to avoid participant fatigue, but you'll also need to give the users time to complete their tasks. You'll also need to leave time between sessions for consolidating your notes and setting up for the next participant.

- You will need to have a test environment set up that the participants have access to. Any technical requirements need to be part of your recruiting *and* your confirmation communications. Making sure your participants are set up and ready to test when the session starts can be a challenge. If there are passwords, special URLs, or test credit/ gift cards, make sure you have all that information communicated in advance and on hand at your session. Any delay in testing can have serious ripple effects in the project schedule.

- With usability testing sessions you should expect to pay your participants. If your target demographic is broad and you can use just about anyone off the street, you should expect to pay $50.00 per participant. I've recently completed a session with high-level software managers and we had to pay $200.00 for each of those participants. The harder they are to find and the more senior they are in their profession, the more they usually cost. Most other aspects of the process are similar to the process of discussing market fit with market representatives.

The Testing Script

SolMon App Survey Draft - 2/15/2020

Thank you for participating in this testing session.

My name is <moderator name> and I will guide you through tasks and will ask for your feedback. Try to follow all instructions carefully and feel free to ask for clarification if you have any questions. Your feedback is very valuable to us. With that in mind please be honest with your feedback. Our feelings won't be hurt by anything you have to say and your honest feedback will help us improve the experience for future users. Also, we are not testing you. We are testing the system you'll use today. If you have trouble with a task for any reason, that may be an indication that we need to make changes.

If you haven't already done so, please make sure to set up your device to be able to access the test site by following these instructions: <link to instructions>

Introductory Questions

Please tell us a little bit about yourself before we begin.

- What is your age?
- How long have you been in the solar industry?
- Are you aware of the SolMon brand?
- Have you used SolMon previously?
- What type of device do you usually use when monitoring the performance of solar installations you are involved with? Please include the model and OS version.
- What software do you use to monitor the performance of solar installations?

OK, let's move on to trying some of the tasks. On your <device type>, open your browser and visit the following URL: uat.solmon.com

Task 1

As you work to complete the tasks in this session, please "think out loud" so I will have a better understanding of what you are thinking at each step of the process. Also, please let me know when you believe you have completed each task.

Starting on the home page, imagine you received an alert showing that the system isn't performing as expected. Please describe and show me how you would proceed to investigate the details of the alert to determine the next steps.

<once the user believes they have completed the task>

Please describe how you were feeling as you worked to complete the task: excited, happy, not really feeling anything, confused, frustrated, or angry.

I'm not going to write out the rest of the questions because there would be a lot of repetition and not much knowledge sharing going on. In general, if your tasks are relatively simple, you can usually have a max of 20 or so in a one-hour session. If the tasks are larger and involve free-roaming exploration, you should probably cut that number to 10. Your best bet is to start with 10 and test yourself. You are going to be faster than the average user, so keep that in mind.

You should also leave time for some wrap-up questions.

Wrap-up Questions

Below are a few final questions. Please base your answers on your overall experiences throughout this session.

What did you like MOST about using the SolMon service?
What did you like LEAST about using the SolMon service?
How likely is it that you would recommend SolMon to a colleague?
0 = Not Likely [#'s] 10 = Very Likely

Are there any comments you would like to share about SolMon or the testing experience today?
Thank you for your participation in this study.

Analysis

Once you have the results from all the sessions you need to complete the analysis, document the observations, and make your recommendations just like the market research part of the project. Make sure to create a brief executive summary so your team can derive some value from the research without much investment of their time. Encourage them to review the report in detail. In some cases, especially when your company is young, you can get the team together for a quick review of the findings so everyone has time to share questions and learn from the work you have done.

The Next Iteration

This next iteration should be a lot easier to plan than the original one was because you have already established the goals, strategies, objectives, etc. Your primary focus at this point is to incorporate the learnings from the usability testing into the work your team has already done. Unless you heard that there is a strong need for a fundamental change in the approach, your team should be feeling pretty good about things and confident that you are all on the right track.

The UI Design

All of the work we have discussed so far has been done with the primary goal of defining what needs to be designed and built before investing too much time and money in things that wouldn't provide value for the users or the company. Working with relatively low-fidelity wireframes and storyboards allows the team to move quickly, test, iterate, and continue doing so until they feel confident they are on the right track. It also allows members of many different teams with different skill sets to take an active part in the process, providing more comprehensive solutions while building consensus.

As we enter the UI design process the work becomes a bit more siloed. The UI designer(s) will be focusing on creating the visual style of the interface. The designers will ensure that the final UI supports the visual hierarchy, branding, content requirements, interactions, and accessibility required to facilitate the intended user experience. Where the wireframe work was fast and loose, UI design is just the opposite. This is the part of the process where the intended experience gets buttoned up and polished to communicate an appropriate amount of professionalism while enhancing the user's ability to scan, read, comprehend, and navigate all the content your service has to offer.

During this phase of the project the development team is usually laying the code-based foundation of the system to support the new UI, and the content teams are putting the final touches on all the copy, images, and video.

The design team will usually present a small number of variations of the UI so the team can provide feedback during a design critique for a round or two of edits before the final version is approved. Keep your critiques focused on business outcomes, not opinions, and keep the feedback positive and actionable to help avoid letting emotion drive your design process.

From there, the very detailed work of documenting the styles and creating all necessary resources to support the future design and development of the system takes place. For more on the details of this process, review Chapter 3, "Make It Beautiful."

Lastly, once the proposed UI is designed, another round of testing with high-fidelity screens or a clickable prototype will help validate the UI and catch any remaining issues so they can be dealt with before the solution is coded.

Development

The development team will likely break down all the required functionality into development stories, including variations for the backend and frontend. If your team is tightly integrated, there may have been design and content stories as well that helped flesh out the development stories.

All those stories will then get scheduled based on priority and complexity. The work will get handed off to various developers and be completed over a fixed period of time, usually defined as a milestone. It is not unlikely that there will be changes along the way because there are two distinct phases of both design and development. The R+D phase is notoriously difficult to schedule, because during that phase your team is at the wide end of the cone of uncertainty. As the work shifts into the production phase, it is much easier to schedule because the work that needs to be done is very well understood at the narrow end of the cone of uncertainty.

Periodically the dev team will typically demo working pieces of functionality to verify that they are on the right track and show progress toward the milestone. Some of these review sessions may be considered to be user acceptance tests, or UAT. The formal version of this would include testing with users who match the target demographic, much like the usability testing in the design phase. In my experience, though, many teams don't test with users at this phase and instead what they call UAT is actually a product team acceptance test. Either way, there is a final review phase where functionality gets demonstrated and/or tested by the product team for them to approve.

Some teams have dedicated QA professionals and for teams like that, the QA team will be providing feedback during the entire design and development process. Other teams will have readiness teams that will coordinate the efforts of all the other teams to ensure that every release has been holistically considered so that all aspects of the customer experience have been accounted for and addressed before the changes go live. Many startup teams lack this level of preparedness, and the QA and readiness tasks fall back onto the UX and product teams. Either way, once that final level of review is complete, the new experience will be scheduled to go live.

Whenever changes are released, it is a good idea to have a system in place to validate the changes were all made as planned and resulted in the expected behaviors within your service. Without these checks in place, it is entirely possible that your efforts will end up hurting the experience instead of helping it. Something as simple as one file not getting updated properly on one of the load-balanced servers can have seriously negative impacts on usage.

If an issue is detected during the system review after pushing changes live, it is a great idea to already have a rollback plan in place to help minimize the time users are negatively impacted by failed releases to decrease the chances that your team will make the situation worse by rushing an unplanned rollback. For more information on this process, review Chapter 4, "Make It Functional."

The Results

As I mentioned before, this is one of the most exciting parts of the entire process. All the hard work your team has put in has manifested itself in a new experience and if all goes requires further discussion, the facilitator should add a blue Post-it arrow to create an action item for that topic to be discussed further at a later date. The Post-it should then be placed back within the section it came from.

That process should continue and complete when all the "what went well" items in the last section are complete. The purpose of this session isn't to resolve any issues that get noted; the purpose is to provide positive feedback and recognition to the team for the items that went well and to improve awareness and consideration of the items that didn't go well. If this session devolves into a solutioning meeting, it could take days and that isn't an efficient use of everyone's time. Team leaders within the organization will be taking the next step of prioritizing issues and working on resolutions.

With everything that was learned from the usage results as well as the information gathered from your postmortem, your team will be ready to leverage what has been learned to iteratively improve during the next round.

Working within an Established Company

The example process I described in the previous section doesn't account for some of the nuance involved in creating great experiences when the organization is so big that you don't know each member of each team. Internal politics, conflicting priorities between corporate divisions, legacy policies, and processes all become factors that need to be accounted for.

This section provides awareness of the most common issues I've encountered, as well as some approaches to dealing with them as you work toward contributing to improved experiences and outcomes.

Getting Up to Speed

Probably the biggest shock to me on a regular basis when working with established companies is how many leaders within the organization cannot communicate clearly what company goals and strategies their teams are working toward. Many times the best information I can get is very tactical and directly related to the short-term items the teams are expected to deliver without a strong connection to a measurable objective outcome. This observation is backed up by the data presented in an article published by the *MIT Sloan Management Review* called "No One Knows Your Strategy—Not Even Your Top Leaders." The authors point out that one study found that only one-quarter of the managers surveyed could list three of the company's five strategic priorities. Even worse, one-third of the leaders charged with implementing the company's strategy could not list even one.

No matter how good you are, you are not going to fix an issue of this scale quickly, but you can and should be part of the solution. This single issue is one of the primary reasons I wrote this book. There is a lot of wasted life going into designing and building useless things all over the world, and the root of that problem starts with company leaders who don't know or cannot communicate the goals, strategies, and objectives that their teams should be working toward.

As you begin your journey working with or within an established company, do your part to identify and document the goals, strategies, and objectives and use them in conversations to help drive the direction of the work you are being asked to do. This is a sensitive topic and needs to be approached with caution. Confronting a team lead in a public forum about their lack of guidance on these topics is going to put everyone in a bad position. A better approach is to ask "How will we know if we have succeeded?" If the person leading the project doesn't have that answer, suggest that another session be set up to help document what criteria will be used to determine if the effort is a success or failure.

This will give the project leader who is ill-prepared the time to get that information without being cornered and exposed. As I've said many times in this book, UX is a team sport and keeping the team moving toward long-term, repeatable success is much more valuable than any short-term personal gain that might come from exposing the short-comings of another team member. Once you have the high-level strategic vision documented, you'll want to tie information back to any current internal benchmarks for the KPIs and metrics.

By now you know I'm skeptical of numbers when they are presented to me. The first time you are introduced to the KPIs and metrics at a new company is a good time to focus and critically think about how these numbers were gathered and whether or not you believe they are accurate. Hopefully the team member that gives you those numbers can share how they were captured and discuss steps that have been taken to ensure that they are reliable. Digging into the numbers early will help by giving you insight into what is being captured and what isn't, as well as getting you familiar with how analysis and reporting works at this new company so you can explore on your own.

Once you have a clear picture of how the high-level goals, strategies, and objectives map to the current performance via KPIs and metrics and have a plan in place to address any shortcomings you found, you can approach understanding the existing UX and design artifacts.

Knowing Your Place on the Team

How the current team works together is very important, and finding a way to integrate yourself seamlessly into the existing process can be a challenge. My recommendation is to set up short meetings with each member of the team with the agenda of getting

To overcome the communication problem I first make sure that I'm overcommunicating from my point of view. So far I haven't had a client state that they wanted me to keep them up to date less than I do, so I haven't overdone that part yet. The exact opposite has happened. I often get thanked for my status updates and not letting issues get out of hand.

The second problem is harder to solve, but my best approach to date for making sure I don't overcommit is to insist that I need to have time to break the problem down so that I can accurately estimate the work. Putting a pause on the estimation process even for a few minutes helps me get out of the "anything is possible" mindset and engage my critical thinking skills to really consider what it will take to get it done, including eating and sleeping.

There are, of course, still times when schedules will slip but when they do, it won't have such a negative impact if you succeeded in improving on the communication side of things and the possibility of slipping was discussed previously and planned for.

Feedback: How to Take It and How to Give It

A very well-respected designer friend once told me that the manager working on a project she created some design work for said, in front of the rest of the team, that the work she presented looked like what his dog left in his yard this morning. She was then and still is one of the best designers I've ever met. She told me that story very early in my career because I was visibly upset about something a client had said to me. I had so much respect for this designer that I knew for sure that what she presented had to have been quality work, and her story helped me understand that sometimes no matter how much work you put in and how well-conceived and executed your design is, you are going to run into a jackass that tries to make you feel bad because they themselves have more "issues" than *National Geographic*.

Aside from being completely unprofessional, the real reason his feedback was terrible is that there was no value in it. His feedback was completely devoid of anything that could be built upon. In order for feedback to be helpful it must be positive, be specific, and include a next step.

Why should feedback be positive?   Because we are all professionals working together toward the same goals. We may not agree on everything, but it is important that we all treat each other with respect as we work to create the best solutions for the companies we work for.

I'm sure there are some that will read this and want to disregard it, but I encourage everyone to recognize that this isn't just my opinion. Google conducted a two-year research project into what helps teams perform well, and according to an article in the *Harvard Business Review* titled "High-Performing Teams Need Psychological Safety,"

Paul Santagata, Head of Industry at Google, says, "There is no team without trust." I would extend that to say that respect is essential as well. In general, we can't feel threatened by members of our own team and work as efficiently as possible because part of our cognitive energy is always going to be focused on protecting us rather than on solving the problem at hand.

Why should feedback be specific?   Because ambiguity leads to misunderstanding, and confusion and forces the team to waste more time seeking clarification.

Why should feedback include a next step?   Because it shows that the person providing the feedback is working as part of the team to move things forward while helping to clarify their concern by providing more context.

Along with providing quality feedback, some other ways to promote psychological safety in your teams are to celebrate successes, honestly and openly recognize failures with the focus on next steps, and emphasize the value of the teamwork in solving the biggest problems.

Working within a Mega-Company

I've consulted at some of the world's biggest and most influential businesses. I differentiate between those that are big and those that are influential because those two things don't always go hand in hand. UpToDate is the number-one clinical information resource for doctors all over the world. It is used in teaching hospitals all over the United States, and if you have gone to the doctor in the past 15 years, you were very likely treated by a physician that uses UpToDate. Unless you are in the medical industry, you likely have never heard of UpToDate, but their influence on the standard of care around the world is undeniable. When I worked there the founder would frequently remind the team that the quality of our work was incredibly important because a mistake that we make today will become the standard of clinical care tomorrow. When you work on systems that impact people's lives all over the world, it forces you to focus at a completely different level.

I've also consulted with Google via Applause as a researcher to help improve systems that are used worldwide, and as one of the world's largest companies they are designing and developing at a scale that I've never encountered anywhere else. Many of their services are used by more than one billion people a month. There were more UX researchers associated with one of the projects I worked on with Google than UX employees of all roles at most other companies. Even with the deep resources Google can leverage, they still need to bring in countless contractors because they have so many initiatives progressing concurrently and because their services reach so many people.

Working at this scale requires discipline and coordination that you simply will not encounter almost anywhere else. Problems at this scale need to be broken down into chunks that can be executed on and planned for. It isn't uncommon to be conducting a

You can't. It is that simple. The best you can do is guess, and if you represent an expert superuser persona of the thing you are trying to build, your guess might hit the nail on the head. It isn't impossible, but it's also not a repeatable process that other teams will be able to learn from and use.

The way it should work is that the design teams should have their own sprints where they specify, design, test, and iterate in the same way the development teams already do. Then once the design process has promoted solutions that have been tested and found to be useful and usable, the work to get those built should be added to the development team's backlog.

Conclusion

Most of the issues I see working with software companies center on what I see as a fundamental problem with how companies are founded. A stereotypical startup will begin with a founder who has an idea. If the founder has enough development skills to build the first version, they will. If they don't, they'll hire a developer to join them and build out the first version. If that first version is compelling enough, they might start getting some users or they might go and try to get some funding.

Either way, in almost all cases that first version serves as a foundation for both the code and the design. Iterations happen to add functionality and resolve bugs. Only the very worst UX issues will get resolved because most founders and developers don't even know what heuristics they should be measuring against. That original version continues to get built upon as the team chases new customers by adding new features.

This type of organic growth continues until either a competitor starts to eat their lunch or their investment team complains that there are fundamental issues that need to be resolved in order to capture more of the market or enter new ones. Somewhere along the line the user experience will get prioritized, and at that time the designer that is brought in will most likely be tasked with very tactical work that is essentially putting lipstick on a pig.

At this stage of the game there is a tremendous investment in the code, and most of the company culture has been built around development processes because up until now they are the only members of the team and they have been there since the very beginning. Those two things conspire against efforts to become a more design-driven organization. I'm sad to say, but my experience is that the UX and design teams at many companies are second-class citizens at best, and even with user data to back their recommendations their work often sits dusty on a shelf, never to be released to the user because of some technical or skill limitation imposed by some of the very earliest decisions made at the company.

I wrote this book because many of the world's biggest brands, including Apple, Google, and Amazon, have shown that being design-driven is the best way to create extraordinarily useful, usable, and beautiful products that customers love. They aren't design-driven because they are big companies. They got to be big companies by being design-driven. My hope is that the tools and processes in this book will help you and your team, regardless of the size, focus on what matters as early as possible, and in doing so build a foundation that is strong enough to support the dreams you have for your business.

Best of luck in all your endeavors, and feel free to reach out on Twitter or LinkedIn to let me know what I got right or wrong in this book so that I can do it better in the next iteration.